WIN AT WORK

Navigate the nasties, get things done and get ahead

SHAUN BELDING

KoganPage

LONDON PHILADELPHIA NEW DELHI

First published in Great Britain and the United States in 2010 by Kogan Page Limited

120 Pentonville Road   525 South 4th Street, #241   4737/23 Ansari Road
London N1 9JN   Philadelphia PA 19147   Daryaganj
United Kingdom   USA   New Delhi 110002
www.koganpage.com   India

© Shaun Belding, 2010

ISBN   978 0 7494 5711 2
E-ISBN   978 0 7494 5914 7

British Library Cataloguing-in-Publication Data

A CIP record for this book is available from the British Library.

Library of Congress Cataloging-in-Publication Data

Belding, Shaun.
    Win at work : navigate the nasties, get things done, and get ahead / Shaun Belding.
        p. cm.
    Includes index.
    ISBN 878-0-7494-5711-2 -- ISBN 978-0-7494-5914-7 (ebk) 1. Success in business. 2. Career development. 3. Employability. I. Title.
    HF5386.B367 2010
    650.14--dc22
                                                              2009048335

Typeset by Jean Cussons Typesetting, Diss, Norfolk
Printed and bound in India by Replika Press Pvt Ltd

Contents

About the author

Shaun Belding is the CEO of The Belding Group of Companies, a performance development company with three divisions that include customer service training, mystery shopping and employee performance measurement. Shaun speaks internationally, and is recognized as one of the leading global experts on customer service, service recovery and building positive workplaces.

You can subscribe to Shaun's weekly newsletter *Winning at Work!* by visiting http://www.beldingskills.com/winning-at-work.htm. You can find out more about his speaking availabilities by e-mailing info@beldingskill.com.

To Margo and Cory
The best part of your journey is just beginning.
Enjoy the ride!

Introduction

Don't let successful people intimidate you. Let them teach you

There was a small manufacturing company in Southampton, England that had been going through some tough times. Revenues were down almost 30 per cent, and every department was feeling the pinch. Jonas, a 24-year-old salesman who had just been called into the president's office, wasn't expecting good news. He was the youngest and least experienced of the four-person sales support team – five-person, if you count the manager who had been laid off two months previously.

Five minutes later, Jonas left the office in shock. Not because he had been let go, but because the president informed him that as of that day, he would be the only one left. They'd had to make some very tough decisions, he'd been told, and could afford only one person in the department. They had felt that he was the one who could best find ways to make a difference during this tough period. His modest salary increased by £10,000.

For anyone who knew Jonas, this good fortune came as no surprise. He was well liked and remarkably good at what he did. That he had a bright future ahead of him was abundantly obvious, and the company would have been foolish to let him get away.

Jonas's story, while inspiring, is not unique. When you follow the paths of people who have achieved significant success at work, you will find that his experience is part of a common theme. Ultimately, it was *something he had done* that had caused his success to happen. There was no luck involved, no invisible hand of fate, no nepotism, no office politics. His fortune was foreseeable and legitimate. On the surface, it might appear that he had defied all odds. Dig a little deeper, though, and you see that he didn't beat the odds, he had *changed* the odds.

It is a poignant illustration of how much control we have over our success in life. We might not be able to influence world events, but we most certainly can exert great influence in our own little parts of the universe. We can impact our families, our friends, our co-workers, our companies, our lives. We have an opportunity, every day, to change the odds in our favour.

Win at Work covers five fundamental topics: The Winning Attitude, Achievement and Success, Winning in the Workplace, Winning with People, and Dealing with Stress and Difficult People. I chose these topics because they are all things that we have real control over. They are things we can influence and improve. It is not intended to be so much of a cohesive, single-focused treatise on workplace success, but rather a compendium of philosophies, principles and practices that successful people share.

My hope is that each reader can find at least one thing that will make his or her little universe a better place. Have fun with *Win at Work*, and may the odds be with you.

Part I

The winning attitude

Open your ears, your mind and your heart.
This is how you open your future

There is a news story about a Master's student in California who was offered a job at the high-tech giant, Cisco. Apparently, right after she hung up the telephone with them she sent the following message via the micro-blog, Twitter: 'Cisco just offered me a job! Now I have to weigh the utility of a fatty pay-check against the daily commute to San Jose and hating the work.'

An hour later, she received this reply: 'Who is the hiring manager? I'm sure they would love to know that you will hate the work. We here at Cisco are versed in the web.' Rumour has it she didn't get the job after all. Surprise, surprise.

The stark reality of life is that it doesn't matter how smart you are, how educated you are, or how talented you are. If your attitude is lousy, so are your chances of achieving any semblance of success. The more you get to meet people who have achieved great things or have reached the pinnacles in their fields, the clearer this becomes. There is a commonality in the way successful people think and the way they look at the world. While they may be very different in discipline, expertise and personality, they have in common a very distinctive *feel*. It's a confidence, a charisma, an aura – a pervasive attitude that good things are going to happen when they are around. A positive attitude. A *winning* attitude.

Similarly, when you meet people whom we might consider unsuccessful – people who are unhappy at their work or generally underachieve – this same winning attitude is consistently and conspicuously absent. It's not a coincidence.

Psychologist Carl Jung defined 'attitude' as: 'readiness of the psyche to act or react in a certain way.' A *winning attitude*, then, might perhaps be best defined as the 'readiness of the psyche to act or react in a manner that creates positive outcomes.' It's one of the primary defining characteristics of highly successful people, and when you begin to scrutinize it, two questions come immediately to mind. The first has to do with causality. Can one's success really be attributed to something as abstract and intangible as a 'winning attitude?' Or is it more likely that a winning attitude is just a pleasant by-product that comes from being successful?

While there is undoubtedly some truth to both assertions, the anecdotal evidence overwhelmingly points to the first – that our attitudes have a direct bearing on both our achievements and success. All you have to do is take a quick poll of employers to understand the importance of attitude. Most will tell you that, when hiring new employees, they live by the mantra: 'Hire the attitude – you can train the rest.' This suggests that attitude plays a role right from the very first interview at the very start of our careers.

The trend continues as we progress in the workplace. Not only are people with positive attitudes more likely to get the job in the first place, they are also the first to be considered for promotions or more interesting positions. It makes sense when you think about it. Take two individuals, each with equal education, experience and skill. Whom would you choose to promote? Most employers will tell you that they look for 'fit' – for someone who will integrate easily into the team. They look for attitude.

The second question takes us into that classic nature–nurture debate. Is a winning attitude something you just have, or is it something you learn? And if it is learnt, is there a point where it's too late to change? If we don't have it now, can we get it, or can one really not teach old dogs new tricks? The good news, as it turns out, is that not only can we work to develop a winning attitude, but with the focus on a few key principles, we can begin to see almost immediate and positive results from our efforts.

A few years ago, our company did some research to see if we could put more substance to this loosely defined *winning attitude*. Over the course of two years, we identified 86 individuals who had attained a high level of business success, and were deemed as having a 'winning attitude' by those around them. We interviewed them to see if we could determine what, if any, common principles, values, beliefs or traits they might share. The exercise gave some wonderful insight into the mindset of successful people.

When the dust had settled, we were able to categorize the 'winning attitude' into five common characteristics. People with the winning attitude:

1. are positive;

2. understand themselves and what's important;

3. believe;

4. continuously improve;

5. have passion.

In the next few chapters we'll examine these characteristics, and take a look at some strategies as to how you can develop and nurture them.

Winning attitude characteristic 1

The positive attitude

Nothing positive ever came from a negative attitude

Nothing says more about the winning attitude than the word 'positive'. The importance of a positive attitude is one of the most widely touted concepts in personal development, and for good reason. In all of the high-achieving individuals we interviewed, it was by far the most dominant characteristic.

The three traits of a positive attitude

The concept of positive attitude is interesting because, while virtually everyone, even across cultures, perceives it in the same way, most people struggle on how to define it. We recognize it when we see it, but have a hard time putting our fingers on its essence. I think the best way to characterize a winning attitude is to put a bit of a Jungian spin on it, and define it as:

'*A consistent focus on positive action and outcomes, and the pursuit of happiness in self and others.*'

This definition is consistent with those behaviours we attribute to a positive attitude and those people we identify as having it. It manifests itself in the following three traits. A person with a positive attitude:

1. focuses on positive events and aspects;

2. focuses on solutions instead of problems;

3. chooses hope over fatalism.

I. Focuses on positive events and aspects

Let's talk for a moment about what 'positive' and 'negative' really are. These concepts – 'positive', 'negative', 'good', 'bad', 'right', 'wrong', etc are most often presented as tangible or absolute values. In truth, of course, they are neither tangible nor absolute. They are simply labels we place on things based on our environment and personal perceptions. Events and actions are not intrinsically good, bad, positive or negative on their own merits, but we deem them as such depending on where we stand. A rainstorm may be a curse to the would-be sunbather, but a blessing to a nearby farmer. An exacting manager may be a nightmare for a lazy employee, but a boon to a CEO trying to grow the business. An economic downturn can mean disaster to a business on the bubble, but create great opportunity for new businesses as the field of competition diminishes. Positive, negative, good and bad are not *facts*, but value judgements created from our own perspectives.

The point is that in almost every aspect of our lives, we apply these labels by either conscious or subconscious *choice*. We can, for instance, choose to view being fired as a negative thing – as a job lost. Or, we can choose to view it as a positive thing – as a chance to find something better. We can be angry that our alarm clock didn't go off, or we can choose to be happy that we got an extra 20 minutes' sleep.

People with positive attitudes choose, as much as possible, to apply positive labels to events and actions. The rained-out sunbather with the negative attitude gets bitter and twisted. The positive one says, 'Well, it looks like I'm finally going to have the opportunity to get to that book I've been wanting to read.' The loss of a business because of a poor economy means despair and failure to a negative attitude. The entrepreneur with the positive attitude accepts Dr Denis Waitley's wisdom that 'there are no mistakes or failures, only lessons', views the event as a learning experience and moves on.

2. Focuses on solutions instead of problems

Things in life don't always go smoothly. No matter how hard we try, how clever we are or how much we plan, projects will go awry, unexpected things will happen, and people you thought you could depend on will let you down. It's easy to become frustrated, discouraged and demotivated when these things happen. Nobody likes to see their efforts thwarted.

A central part of a positive attitude, however, is the ability to move quickly from problem identification mode to problem-solving mode. People with a positive attitude don't waste time dwelling on negative events, or spend time seeking out who to blame. They focus instead on how best to deal with issues and move beyond them to something more productive.

The following is an example of how people with negative and positive attitudes might approach the same situation.

Negative attitude: The computers went down today and everything ground to a halt.

Negative attitude: The computers went down today, once again exposing how horrible and antiquated our system is.

Positive attitude: The computers went down today, and I think we've just seen how a new system will pay off for us.

It's not that people with positive attitudes don't experience challenges in life. They just choose 'finding a solution' as their first response. While the person with the negative attitude has a sleepless night thinking about all of the consequences and complications that a problem creates, the person with the positive attitude loses sleep thinking of different ways he might be able to fix it. They both lose a night's sleep, but by morning only one is closer to a resolution.

3. Chooses hope over fatalism

There is a very common strategy used by a great many people when approaching a task or awaiting results. It goes something like this: 'I always assume the worst will happen. That way I never get disappointed. Should something good happen instead, then I'm pleasantly surprised.' It's kind of the 'I like to continually beat my head on a hard surface, because it feels so good when I stop' approach to life.

It is true that if you set your standard low enough you never have to deal with unpleasant surprises. But you have to admit that this kind of fatalism is a rather sad way to live one's life. People with positive attitudes always hope for the best. Hope gives us energy and makes our daily lives a lot more pleasant. Yes, sometimes it can hurt when you hope for the best and bad things end up happening, but a positive attitude is what helps you get past those moments. Advertising icon Leo Burnett summed it up nicely when he said, 'When you reach for the stars you may not quite get one, but you won't come up with a handful of mud either.'

Attitude check

Do you have a positive attitude? Here are five questions you should ask yourself from time to time:

1. Do you typically look for what's right, or what's wrong? When things change, are you looking for the good things to come, or do you dwell on the things you've lost? Do you seek ways to enjoy the things you have, or lament the things you don't have? Remember that the way you look at things is a matter of choice, and that no one ever achieved happiness by focusing on the dark side of life.

2. Do you find yourself using a lot of sarcasm? A little well-placed facetiousness can actually be a healthy thing. It's a sign that you're looking at things from different points of view and not just blindly accepting the status quo. If you find yourself in a pattern of using sarcasm frequently, however, it's a red flag that you're choosing to view a significant portion of your life from a negative perspective. That's not a good thing.

3. Do people occasionally tell you to 'lighten up', 'take a pill', 'relax' or to stop being so intense? Sometimes we can take ourselves *way* too seriously. When people start making these comments to you, it can be a sign that you're too self-focused. It's time to step back and look at things from a different perspective. As we'll discuss in the winning with people section, the ability to walk on the lighter side of life goes a long way to building relationships.

4. Do you laugh out loud at least once a day? Closely related to point 3 above, laughter is a good indicator of your attitude. It doesn't count, of course, if the only things you laugh at are sarcastic comments or when other people hurt themselves. If you're not finding opportunities to laugh each day, you're missing out on a lot. Funny things happen all around us all the time – you just have to look for them to see them.

5. Do you find yourself frequently making judgemental comments about the people around you? If you do, it's valuable to ask yourself the follow-up question, 'Why do I do this?' If you're honest with yourself, the answers you generate can go a long way to understanding your own attitudes, and changing them to ones that are more positive and productive. Judgemental attitudes and negative thoughts about others are often created from our own insecurities. You will find that the more confident you become in yourself, the more accepting you become of the frailties of those around you.

If you find that some of these questions hit close to home, take heart. It's not uncommon for even the nicest of people to fall unconsciously into negative attitude patterns. What's important is that we learn to recognize it when it happens, and take steps to correct it. The payoff is huge. If you would like to take a more in-depth look at your attitude, you can take the free test at: www.beldingskills.com/attitude-check.htm.

The relationship between positive attitude and success is irrefutable, and interestingly, not just a one-way street. While all of the high achievers we interviewed attributed a large part of their success to their positive attitude, they also agreed that having success has helped to reinforce their attitude. As one put it, 'Having a positive attitude helps get you where you want to go. But it's also easier to have a positive attitude when things are going well.'

2

Winning attitude characteristic 2

Understanding yourself and what's important

Discovering your true priorities is like an explorer finding True North. Once you have that unchanging frame of reference, reaching any destination you choose only requires a look at your compass, a good map, and a willingness to begin the journey

We were in the last few days of an employee satisfaction and internal customer service audit with a large service organization. It was our 22nd focus group, and it consisted of six senior managers. One of the managers – we'll call her Susan – began telling us of her management philosophy. 'I believe in creating a respectful environment', she said. 'I like to get input from everyone and get everyone involved. We have a very happy and close-knit team.' Out of the corner of my eye, I caught one of the other managers in the room almost choking on the muffin he was eating.

I had to struggle to maintain a poker-face as well. The speaker was the same manager who had been identified in a half-dozen other focus groups as one of the greatest sources of stress in the organization. Less than two hours earlier I had heard of an episode which featured her standing in the middle of an open work area, loudly screaming at an entire data-input team.

Several months later, and to Susan's disbelief, she was fired for 'failing to create a positive work environment'. She felt vilified, and filed a wrongful dismissal suit which she later dropped on her own lawyer's advice.

Susan's somewhat distorted self-perception is not unusual. Most of us have met at least one person whose self-image bears very little resemblance to reality. They'll tell you all kinds of things about themselves: 'I'm a very honest person', 'I'm very thorough', 'I'm very organized', 'I have an excellent memory' – but you know from experience that these statements don't really hold up to close scrutiny. We're all guilty of this to some extent, of course. We all have shortcomings we don't recognize, and we all think we have strengths that just aren't there. Instead of active pursuit to be the person we aspire to be, we too frequently delude ourselves into believing we've already arrived.

One of the most significant characteristics of highly successful people is that they have a pretty clear idea of who they really are. They understand their strengths, and aren't afraid to acknowledge their imperfections. Because their self-perception is less distorted than most, they're in a better position to make changes to improve who they are and what they do. It's not a very common trait, and to be honest, it's not an easy thing to do. It takes courage to look in the mirror and face our inner demons. It also requires a belief that having defects doesn't necessarily make someone defective. Having flaws, after all, is not a statement against your character. It's a statement of your humanity.

Know your priorities

Part of understanding who you are includes having a very clear idea of what is truly important to you. Individuals with the winning attitude understand their priorities, and use them as their guidelines when making decisions. Because their actions are in line with these priorities, they inevitably get greater enjoyment out of the things they do.

Just as most of us haven't spent adequate time assessing ourselves and our actions, most of us also haven't spent nearly enough time reflecting on the things in life that are truly important to us. The unfortunate effect of this is that we can find ourselves doing things that may seem like a good idea at the time, but ultimately end up compromising both our success and our happiness. How many times have we heard stories of people we consider tremendously successful who turn out to be profoundly unhappy? We hear of people making horrible sacrifices to get to where they are – only to discover that it really just wasn't worth it.

The tabloids might have you believe it's an affliction restricted to the rich and famous, but it's a part of most of our lives. We all make decisions that we regret later. We miss a child's piano recital because we have to work late. We spend money on our upgraded cable TV, but can't afford the trip to visit an ailing relative. We continue to work for an unethical boss because the pay is so good. We pursue the wrong things for the wrong reasons, which invariably takes us down paths we really don't want to be on.

To avoid this trap, it is an invaluable exercise to take the time to reflect on what your priorities actually are. If you want to be serious about it, sit down some evening and make a list of the things in life that are really important to you. What are the things you like doing? What are the types of accomplishments that truly make you proud? What are the things that define who you are and the person you would like to be?

Make sure the list comes from the heart (no one is going to read it but you). It's a common mistake when doing this exercise for us to identify things we think *should* be our priorities, instead of what they really are. We might write down things like 'Family', or 'Helping the environment', because they are generally accepted important values. This ends up being counterproductive, of course, if they really aren't that important to you.

Once you have your list, ask yourself the following questions: Based on what I've just written down, am I actually doing the things that are really important to me? Are my actions generally in line with my priorities? If you answer no to either, then your next step is to take action to correct it.

This, as it turns out, is the really hard part. Change isn't easy for any of us – even at the best of times. Trying to realign your actions to your priorities is tough, particularly if you've been walking down the wrong path for any length of time. Sometimes it can mean giving up quite a lot.

One of the most poignant examples of this came from a Senior Vice President in our survey group who confided that she paid her way through university as an exotic dancer. One of the hardest decisions she ever made, she said, came after graduation. She was offered a full-time job in a junior marketing position with a large company. While the opportunities for advancement were good, the starting salary was just $22,000 – a far cry from the $60,000+ she was currently making in her part-time job. She took the job, quit dancing, sold her Jaguar, and moved from her three-bedroom downtown condo into a one-bedroom flat in the suburbs. 'It was Hell for the first year', she said, 'but I was finally able to look in the mirror and see a future.'

The ultimate payoff to understanding your priorities and letting them guide your decisions and actions is undeniable. The more your actions begin to align with those things you feel are important, the greater your satisfaction and success.

Put things into perspective

Knowing who you are and what your priorities are gives you confidence in yourself and your decisions. It also helps you better put the challenges you face into proper perspective, which is one of the best ways to make sure that you're mentally prepared for the things life throws at you. When you have a solid understanding of the things that are truly important, they become the benchmark by which you determine the importance of the events that happen around you. That way, when you find yourself getting really stressed at work or at home, whether it's a time crunch, a workload issue or a people problem, it's easier to answer the following questions:

1. In the scheme of things, how important is this really?

2. Five years from now, how much of an impact will this have made on my life?

3. Is this really a potentially life-altering moment (and if not, then why am I getting stressed over it)?

4. What's the worst that could happen? And is the 'worst case' really a bad thing (eg maybe losing this job wouldn't be the end of the world)?

These are critical internal questions that we need to ask every time we find ourselves becoming stressed or apprehensive about something. When we take the time to actually answer them, we discover that the majority of things that keep us up at night aren't really so terrible after all. High achievers excel in typically stressful situations in part because they are able to put events and situations into proper perspective. Their perspective helps them understand the real risks involved, and the degree to which events will actually impact them.

Integrity check

Integrity is one of the dominant values of high achievers, and another core component of the winning attitude. People respect people with integrity. This respect, in turn, opens doors for opportunity. And opportunity, of course, is the lifeblood of achievement. Conversely, should someone perceive you as having a lack of integrity, it will ultimately diminish your opportunities for success. The fundamental meaning of integrity is 'wholeness', or 'completeness'. In essence, as it relates to character, it means that all of your thoughts and actions are consistent with the kind of person you think you are or would like to be. It means you walk your proverbial talk.

One of the exercises we do in our leadership workshops is to ask participants to rate themselves on their integrity. The scale is 1 to 10, with 1 being no integrity and 10 being the highest degree of integrity possible. On average, participants consistently rate themselves between 8 and 10. In almost 20 years of asking this question, we have never had a participant give themselves below a 7.

This tells us that everyone recognizes the importance of integrity, and that everyone aspires to it. The quality is clearly valued by everyone. Virtually everyone changes their score, however, after they review a brief integrity checklist. See how *you* score on the five simple questions on the following page.

Give yourself five points for every a) you selected, two points for a b), one for a c) and zero for a d). If you get 17–25 points, then you're on the right track. If you get 10–17 points, you may want to take a closer look at your actions and how others may be perceiving you. If you get fewer than 10 points, you need to go out and get a big stick, then whack yourself about the head with it.

Your Integrity Checklist

1. I do the things I say I'm going to do
    a) Without exception
    b) With one or two exceptions
    c) 50/50
    d) Rarely

2. I never say anything behind someone's back that I wouldn't say to their face
    a) Without exception
    b) With one or two exceptions
    c) 50/50
    d) I am frequently guilty of this

3. I don't tell lies or 'stretch the truth'
    a) Without exception
    b) With one or two exceptions
    c) 50/50
    d) I often stretch the truth

4. I don't do things against my better judgement just because it makes things easier
    a) Without exception
    b) With one or two exceptions
    c) 50/50
    d) I frequently give in

5. I will never divulge something told to me in confidence
    a) Without exception
    b) With one or two exceptions
    c) Only when it's important
    d) Don't tell me any secrets

Integrity is all about aligning your self-perception with reality, and your words with your actions. Most of us aren't nearly as good at this as we would like to be, which is why people with high integrity levels stand out so much. The vast majority of us compromise our integrity with alarming frequency. We make little promises and commitments, then don't keep them. We exaggerate, or 'stretch the truth' to make our points. We give in to peer pressure and do things we know aren't quite right. The result is an inadvertent, and generally unacknowledged, compromise in integrity.

So how is it that most people will claim integrity as one of their core values, yet can so easily cast it aside when it suits them? The answer is that most of us simply haven't thought it through. The ability to maintain your integrity requires, above all, the ability to be as honest with yourself as you can. The problem is that most of us just aren't introspective enough to actually realize the damage we do to ourselves and our reputation. We don't see the things we do and say that undermine our own credibility. To make matters worse, very few people – certainly not our friends – will actually take us to task on our integrity issues, so we end up continuing our self-sabotaging behaviour, perfectly content in our delusions.

Your internal devil's advocate

One of the best practices you can develop to help you to avoid falling into the trap of self-delusion is to have a little part of your brain allocated to play the role of 'Devil's Advocate'. This is the little person in your head who will stand up and challenge your own self-beliefs. So the next time you say something like, 'I'm a very organized person', the little voice pops into your head that says, 'Oh yeah? What about the time that you...'. It's quite enlightening when you have the courage to let this thought process take place. You begin to get a clearer picture of your relationship with the world around you and where your opportunities and challenges really are.

The most successful people you will ever meet have a strong sense of who they are. They know what strengths they can leverage and what weaknesses they need to improve or compensate for. They understand what is important to them, and use that as a compass to direct their thoughts and actions. As much as possible, they don't allow self-delusion to influence them.

People with this aspect of the winning attitude, who understand who they are and what's important to them, are instantly recognizable. They are the people who seem to exude confidence and strength of character. They are the people who have a *presence* whenever they enter a room.

These characteristics are quite attainable. All it takes is the willingness and courage to take an honest look at yourself, your beliefs, values and perspectives. The next, more difficult step is to actually make the kinds of changes you need to make to move your values, thoughts and actions into alignment. How do you know when you've accomplished this? You'll know. You'll feel confident, relaxed and comfortable. It's well worth the effort.

3

Winning attitude characteristic 3

Believing

Too many people do nothing, then lament what could have been

A lot has been said over the years about the benefits of believing in yourself and positive self-talk. It's not a new concept, of course. Anyone who ever read the 1930 Watty Piper children's classic, *The Little Engine That Could*, knows the benefits of believing in yourself. How can anyone forget the engine's wonderful mantra changing from 'I think I can, I think I can' to 'I know I can, I know I can'?

I'm often surprised, however, at how frequently I hear people convincing themselves that they *can't* do something. When faced with a new challenge, they lament that they don't know how to do it. They stress and worry and fret that they're going to mess up on a project or task. They don't speak up in meetings because they're afraid their ideas might get shot down. Their fear of failure completely overshadows their belief in their own abilities.

Here's my question: What is there to not believe in?

Assuming that you've done the due diligence of knowing who you are and what your priorities are; assuming that you're competent and intelligent – what is there to not believe in? One of the hallmarks of people with the winning attitude is that they don't get caught in the negative self-talk trap. When action needs to be taken, they give it their best shot. They try. They don't always succeed, but they always try. They believe in *possibilities*, and look for ways to make things work.

Accept responsibility

In order to achieve this level of confidence in your abilities, there are a number of things you have to do. The first is to accept responsibility for your own future. People with the winning attitude universally agree that they are ultimately accountable for both their successes *and* their failures.

High-performing individuals don't readily accept concepts of fate or luck. They adhere to deterministic beliefs such as expressed in the quote attributed to Thomas Jefferson, 'I'm a great believer in luck, and I find the harder I work, the more I have of it.' This attribute is significant, because it differs greatly from the belief structure most people have. Most of us place far too much weight in luck, fate and inevitability. We resign ourselves to accepting the Bad Things that happen to us. We allow external events to influence and shape our lives and our happiness, instead of taking control and creating our own path.

If we are to be honest with ourselves, we have to admit that this belief structure is the easy way out. After all, as long as we can blame 'bad luck', or 'it just wasn't meant to be' for our failures, then failure becomes far less painful. It's easy consolation when we can convince ourselves that we're just helpless pawns in a larger game. The problem with this fatalistic attitude, of course, is that it becomes much more difficult for us to feel good about our successes. After all, we can't very well claim credit for our success if we don't also accept responsibility for our failures.

Don't get me wrong. I'm not suggesting that there is no luck, or some degree of fate in our lives. It's just that individuals with the winning attitude don't believe in waiting passively for luck or fate to dictate their success. They accept responsibility for both their actions and inactions, and recognize the degree in which both influence their lives.

Here's a little exercise we do in our leadership workshops. We show the following five statements on a slide, and then ask participants to see if they can identify the limiting common denominator in all five. See if you can spot it:

1. I've talked with Susan 15 times about this, and she's still not doing it.

2. It seems like I'm always having to make an exception for Fred.

3. Susan is the most unmotivated person I know.

4. Fred is so darned negative all the time.

5. Susan doesn't have the skill to get to the next level.

It typically takes a few minutes and a number of broad hints before someone picks out the common denominator. (The first guess is invariably that Susan and Fred should have been fired long ago. Probably accurate, but that's not the point!) The common theme in each of these is that the person speaking has completely abdicated any responsibility for Susan and Fred's behaviour. The statements tell us that the problem is with Fred and Susan, and doesn't even hint at the possibility that the root issue might be a little closer to home – with our leadership skills. Obvious? Perhaps. But how many times have we all been guilty of pointing fingers at others when they really should have been pointed at us?

People with the winning attitude look differently at the challenges that surround them. They always look to themselves first when diagnosing a situation. Take a look at the exact same issues, and how someone with the winning attitude might frame them:

1. I haven't applied any consequences to Susan's performance.

2. I'm not setting a standard and sticking to it.

3. I haven't figured out how to motivate Susan yet.

4. I haven't effectively expressed to Fred that I expect positive behaviour.

5. I haven't given Susan enough tools to get to the next level.

In this second set of statements, the speaker has identified himself as the cause of each issue. He now has claimed at least some degree of control over Susan's and Fred's actions, and in doing so has given himself the power to improve things. Quite a difference from the powerlessness of the initial statements, which left the outcomes of the situations completely at the mercy of Fred and Susan.

Personal power and the blame game

You don't have to be in a management position for the winning attitude to make a difference to you. In fact, people's attitudes towards responsibility and control are a common issue in a great many organizations. Our company does a lot of work with organizations who are looking to improve their internal customer service and overall morale. Often the challenges they're dealing with in the workplace have been caused by internal changes, such as rapid growth, corporate mergers, downsizing or restructuring.

When faced with these tumultuous situations, it's not uncommon for employees, particularly those who are not in management positions, to feel a significant amount of discomfort. They are unsure of their new roles, new expectations, and their abilities to meet them. Often they are concerned about whether they will even have jobs in the near future. They feel lost, and powerless to change or influence their situation. This frustration, when left unaddressed, inevitably leads to apathy, disenchantment and an ultimate loss of productivity.

It's not an issue restricted to companies undergoing change, of course. This kind of stress can also occur in a very stable company where management has been neglectful of the employee environment. Typically a company doesn't even realize it's happening until it begins to see a spike in employee turnover. In exit interviews, HR managers hear the same story over and over again: It's them, management, who aren't looking after things. *Them.* Once again blame is shifted, and power is lost.

It's unfortunate, because what many people lose sight of is that the power to influence our surroundings has less to do with our *positions* within an organization, and more to do with our *dispositions*. We don't actually lose our power, as much as we give it away. This is done, to a great extent, by playing the blame game.

Consider the middle manager who's been charged with implementing a change in process. He approaches his employees, beginning with, 'OK, this is what *they* want us to do...' Think about the message this sends to the employees. By not championing or taking ownership of situations, he has just positioned himself as powerless within the organization. If that is indeed the case, why on earth should employees be inclined to respect him or respond to him?

Consider the customer service employee who's dealing with an upset customer. She explains to the customer, 'I know it's frustrating, but that's the way *they* want us to do it...' Having just been told by the employee herself that she has no power, why would a customer not be inclined to escalate an issue to someone with greater authority?

Consider the co-worker who regularly complains about the stupid things *they* do. Again, the message is that he is completely at the mercy of a bunch of stupid people. Hmm. What does it say about the person who chooses to work for them?

Blame is a wonderful thing. It makes us feel better when we can convince ourselves that we're smarter than the people around us. (After all, if we were in charge, we wouldn't be making all of these obvious mistakes, would we?) And let's face it: as long as we have someone else to blame for our woes, we don't have to feel responsible for fixing things, do we?

Casting blame, however, while perhaps giving us some short-term satisfaction, has serious negative implications for our long-term opportunities and happiness. It disempowers us and tells everyone around us that we are not willing to take responsibility for those things within our control. The winning attitude means looking past failures, and towards opportunities and ways to make things better. Here's a great rule to live by: Champion it, fix it or leave it. Blame is a game for the uninspired.

Opportunity is everywhere

It really is a shame that there are so many people who spend such extraordinary amounts of time and energy lamenting their fate, and trying to convince others (and themselves) that the world is against them. If they spent just half that energy seeking and seizing opportunity, they would be a lot happier and a lot better off.

Malcolm Gladwell, in his bestselling book *Outliers*, illustrates the pivotal role that opportunity has played in the success of some of the world's most successful people. One of his more poignant examples is that of Bill Gates, founder of the ubiquitous Microsoft Corporation. Contrary to the popular folklore surrounding him, Mr Gates wasn't just a brilliant university drop-out who happened to make it big. He was a young man, enthralled by computers, who took advantage of a confluence of opportunities that allowed him to realize his dreams.

Opportunity is a wonderful thing, and the best part is that it's everywhere. It's not reserved for the rich, powerful or smart. It's all around us and there for the taking. You just have to know how to look for it. The ability to see and take advantage of opportunity comes with three things – education (formal and informal), initiative and awareness. And each of these is readily available to anyone willing to make the investment. Education takes time and commitment, initiative takes courage, and awareness takes focus. The rest is easy.

Consider these four scenarios:

1. Two men go to a rummage sale. One picks up an old dusty vase ticketed at $20, then sets it down feeling it's not worth the price. The other picks it up, recognizes it as a valuable antique, and gladly pays for it – selling it days later for a hundred times the price paid.

2. A stranger is seated between two unemployed women in an aeroplane, and says 'hello' to each. One woman chooses to ignore him and engross herself in her book. The other woman strikes up a conversation, and discovers that he is the recruiting manager for a large company who just happens to have a perfect job for her.

3. Two birds stand on a branch over a wormhole. One becomes distracted by a distant noise and turns its head just as the worm appears. The other swoops down and has its breakfast.

4. Two young computer programmers have the opportunity to work on some of the most sophisticated equipment in the world. One sees it as just a job, and rarely shows up early or leaves late. The other spends night and day there, excited by what he can do with these marvellous machines; and the experience helps him in his future creation of Microsoft Corporation.

Are these just examples of good luck? Perhaps. But the winning attitude suggests otherwise. Opportunity is indeed everywhere – but the rest is up to you.

4

Winning attitude characteristic 4

Continuous improvement

> *Everyone around you can be your teacher,*
> *if you allow yourself to always be a student*

Ask any experienced trainer to pick out the individuals in a workshop who are least likely to succeed in the long run, and the answer will always be the same. It's the people who come up to them during the break and say: 'I've been doing this for 20 years. I've seen everything and done it all. I should probably be *teaching* this class...' It's a remarkably accurate red flag for identifying individuals who have exhausted their potential.

The people who rise to the top of their occupations never stop learning. Equally important is that they make a concerted effort to practise their skills until they've mastered them, and then keep practising so they don't fall into bad habits. If you took Latin in school, you'll likely remember your teacher driving home the message – *Repetitio est mater studiorum* ('Repetition is the Mother of Study').

High achievement is an ongoing process. On the road to success, people with the winning attitude don't ever get the feeling that they've *arrived*. They don't view success as a destination, but rather as the journey itself. Individual successes and triumphs are simply viewed as stepping stones on the journey. High achievers are always on the lookout for better ways to do things, because they recognize that the world around them is not standing still.

In 1996, we were working with a large telecommunications provider, and I had the pleasure of meeting a young man who was just beginning his career in sales. He was bright, eager and able to master some fairly complex skills with remarkable ease. By the time he had worked for the company for nine months, he was the top salesperson for his region. By the second year, he was promoted to regional sales manager. In 2002, he accepted a job as Director of Sales & Operations for a national Canadian retailer.

During this six-year span, I probably spoke with him at least once a month. He would call for pointers, ideas, information. He always began his call with, 'Hi, it's Craig. What's next?' It became a game of sorts. I would try to come up with new goals for him, and he would see how quickly he could accomplish them. I was convinced that this young man was going to go anywhere he chose – a conviction only strengthened when I discovered that I was just one of a dozen people to whom he made those phone calls.

In the spring of 2006, at the tender age of 30, he became executive vice president of a multinational electronics company. I still hear from him, albeit now only four times a year or so, but the question is always the same: 'What's next?' Our relationship is definitely not one-way. While I've been a mentor to him, he's been a constant inspiration and role model to me.

This kind of continuous improvement is more than just a process of adding to your body of knowledge. It's really more about gaining *wisdom*. The distinction is important, because just becoming more knowledgeable isn't enough.

Wisdom is everywhere

When we look to further our education or skills, we look to colleges, universities and training companies. We read books, magazines, newsletters; watch videos; or turn to our favourite search engine. In today's information-rich world, virtually everything we might want to know is available if we look in the right places. Education and skills alone, however, are not always enough to ensure the achievement and success one might be seeking in life. The key ingredient is wisdom.

There is a significant difference between education and wisdom. Where education can help you know the right choices to make, wisdom is actually making the right choices. An educated person, for example, may know that exercise is good for him, yet still choose not to exercise. A wise person armed with the same knowledge will choose otherwise. Most of us have met educated people whom we would not consider wise, as well as some very wise people who were not highly educated. Wisdom is the difference between knowing something and truly understanding it.

But where does this wisdom come from? How does one attain it? It's been said that wisdom comes with age and experience, but it's more than that. There are plenty of old and experienced fools around. The answer, and the wonderful thing about wisdom, is that it's everywhere. You don't have to look far to find it. You do have to look, though, and that's the trick.

The key to gaining wisdom is awareness – awareness of the things around you and the people around you. Observe people who are achieving the type of success you would like to have. Watch what they do, how they do it, when they do it, and who they do it with. Then watch people who struggle, or those who never seem to attain what they are seeking. Pay close attention to the difference between the two, and let your actions be guided accordingly.

Don't restrict your observation just to people at work or people in high places. Some of the greatest wisdom you can acquire will come from the unlikeliest of sources – children, casual acquaintances, strangers, pets, wildlife – pretty much anywhere you can imagine. You just have to keep your mind and eyes open. Robert Fulghum, in his classic, *All I Really Need to Know I Learned in Kindergarten*, highlights this beautifully.

5

Winning attitude characteristic 5

Passion

*When you're truly passionate about something,
work ceases to be work*

Whether they are professional athletes, CEOs or street sweepers, people who excel at what they do truly enjoy their jobs. They are, without exception, proud of what they do and how well they do it. Their attitude is simple: if you don't love your job, or aren't proud of what you do, then why would you do it? It's a very good question, and one that people don't ask of themselves often enough.

My brother-in-law, Tim, is VP Global Sales for a large academic publishing company. For as long as I've known him, he's been in sales, and I'm quite sure I've never met anyone who enjoys the selling process more. I can't begin to count the hours we have spent over the years – often into the small hours of the morning – discussing selling strategies, best practices, techniques and faux pas. His passion is palpable, and you can't help but get energized just listening to him. He stands out heads and tails in a profession that most people enter by chance and stay in because they don't know what else to do. It's not an accident he's been successful.

Take a look around your workplace – any workplace. How often do you see people who seem genuinely excited about their job or their company? Not very often. More likely, you hear people quipping 'Thank God it's Friday', or carrying around mugs with 'I Hate Mondays' printed on them. Why is this? Do so many people really hate their jobs?

The answer to this is twofold. The first answer is just a simple yes. Studies around the world tell us that an embarrassingly large portion of the population is genuinely unhappy at work. They're stressed, underappreciated, and feel unfulfilled. The second reason that people don't exhibit passion about their work is a little more insidious, and has to do with the social norms and expectations in the workplace. In many organizations, perhaps even most organizations, it's just not cool to be passionate.

Rob was one of four salespeople who worked for Johnson's Furniture (not the real name), a family-owned furniture manufacturer. Like the others, he had his set accounts, and worked on straight commission. Unlike the others, however, he always made a point of helping out with all the other things that went on in the office. Whenever Mr Johnson needed a hand with anything, Rob was there for him. He would often work long after his shift was over to help out. He didn't get compensated for it, but he truly loved the furniture business, and was eager to learn as much as he could. Needless to say, Mr Johnson genuinely appreciated Rob's effort and initiative, and when a new, more senior position opened up in the office, it was his.

On the surface, everything seemed rosy, but the road to success for Rob wasn't quite as easy as it appeared. The other salespeople hadn't been impressed with Rob's initiative, and he had been taunted daily for his 'brown-nosing' and 'sucking up'. They were annoyed with all the special treatment Rob had received, and took to calling him 'Rob Johnson' in reference to how close he had become to the owner.

It was tough for Rob, because it put him on the outside looking in with his peers. He was rarely invited to any of his colleagues' social events, and they would often do things behind his back. Fortunately, Rob was strong enough to withstand the peer pressure, where most would undoubtedly have succumbed. It is a great illustration of the strong gravitational pull towards mediocrity that we all have to battle.

The challenge in the work environment is that, while you want to fit in, you also want to stand out. Sometimes these two things seem incompatible, and in truth, they are. The secret to overcoming this is to make sure you have a good idea who you want to fit in with. We'll talk more about the importance of surrounding yourself with good people in Chapter 9.

Passion requires courage. It requires the ability to tune out all the negative influences, and focus on something you really enjoy. The great thing is that passion is its own reward. If you have something at work that you're passionate about, don't be afraid to let it show. If you don't have anything you're passionate about, find something. And if you can't find something, well, maybe you need to look for a line of work that does offer something which will inspire the passion within you. To the best of my knowledge, we're not going to get a second chance at this life – so you might as well make the most of things now!

Part 2

Achievement and success

If it hasn't been said, say it. If it hasn't been built, build it. If it hasn't been dreamt of, dream it

Beginning the journey

One of the questions we ask participants in our teambuilding and leadership workshops is, 'Do you genuinely want to be successful?' The universal answer, as you would expect, is a resounding 'Yes'. Interestingly, however, when the same people are asked to define success, virtually all struggle for the answer. Most of us, it seems, are looking for something more and better – but we're just not quite sure what it is we want more and better of. It's like we're all driving a car, not knowing where we are or where we're going – but we're desperately hoping that we get there soon.

A big part of the winning attitude, as we discussed, is having a clear grasp of who you are and what your priorities are. This is a necessary first step, because without this understanding the chances of you truly being successful are remote. Similarly, if you've never taken the time to identify what you want out of life, how would you ever know if you've got it? The better you understand this, the clearer your path becomes. This is the next part of the journey.

What success isn't

What is success? Perhaps the best approach is to start with what it isn't. There are three great myths about success that prevent the vast majority of people from truly enjoying themselves at work and at home.

Myth 1: Success and financial wealth are the same thing

This is the Great Trap. Many people mistake attaining financial wealth and material things for achieving success – then make themselves miserable in the pursuit of them. To be fair, it's an easy mistake to make because financial wealth and success are very often linked quite closely. What people confuse, however, is the causal relationship. Are people successful because they have money, or has their financial wealth come from being successful at what they do? It's an interesting philosophical question, and not everyone, of course, will agree on the answer. But I suspect that if you were to ask Bill Gates, Warren Buffet, Oprah Winfrey or JK Rowling to define what success means to them, their answers wouldn't be 'money'.

Don't get me wrong, I'm not suggesting that money is evil or something that we shouldn't have. It's just that, when we take the time to dig a little deeper, we find that it's not really a bunch of printed pieces of paper that we want. What we're really looking for is something that the money represents to us or brings to us.

Perhaps for you, success means respect, freedom, control of your destiny, security, etc. Financial wealth can be a part of all of these aspirations. The important distinction in all of these is that money isn't the end itself, but either the means to an end or a pleasant by-product.

Myth 2: Success is only attainable for a few

This is nonsense, yet far too many people use this as an excuse for not even trying. The truth is that the only people who can't attain success are either those who haven't defined what success is for them, or those who have defined success in terms that are absolutely unrealistic. It is really the opposite that is true – success is only *unattainable* for a few.

Myth 3: Success comes at a price

It is true that if you define success as being financial wealth, as we discussed above, there can be a terrible price when you sacrifice the things that are truly important to you to achieve that goal. But if you've sacrificed the things that are important to you, have you really achieved success?

The secret to being successful is knowing that there is no secret. It begins with identifying what success means to you – then working towards it with focus and determination. Success isn't an end result that can be measured by others, but a state of mind that can only be measured by you. It's knowing that you're achieving something that is important to you. It doesn't matter whether you've defined success as being a great parent, a leader of industry, a role model for youth, an innovator or just a good friend. What matters is that the definition works for you.

This is where the journey to success begins – with a definition. Before you begin your journey, take the time to gain a clear understanding of what really has to happen in your life for you to consider yourself *successful*. Don't get discouraged if, after reflection, you find yourself struggling to define it in any substantive way. That's part of the process. Just give it your best shot, then set out to achieve it. If you start to find the journey unenjoyable, or that you're paying 'too great a price', then revisit your definition and adjust your course. Nowhere is it written that our journeys have to be in a straight line.

Aligning personal success with business success

It's all very well and good to talk about defining success in our personal lives, but how does this apply to work? If I define success as 'freedom', for example, how does this relate to my job? The answer is that it had better relate to your job, or you're destined to be miserable at work. Just because you do different things in your job from those you do at home doesn't mean that you're a different person. Your core remains the same, and everything you do should stem from that.

But do we really have that much control, you might ask? Aren't our goals at work often set for us? The answer is yes... and no. Take this scenario as an example: A boss had asked two assistants each to prepare a report for an upcoming meeting. One assistant did the work, double-checked the spreadsheets, and printed and stapled eight copies for each person attending the meeting. The other assistant did the same things, but personalized each copy by adding material and an analysis relevant to each person. Both assistants did the job, but one took ownership and tried to add value to the work she did. In doing so, she positioned herself better for future opportunity. If this assistant had identified 'security' as part of her definition of success, then she had moved a step forward. After all, if the boss had to let one of his assistants go, which would he be most likely to choose?

In this section we'll be outlining some effective strategies and principles that can help you navigate your way through the workplace. It's not intended to be an exhaustive list, but it does represent the types of approaches that are required to achieve any sort of success.

One important note before we move on: success is not a static thing. The way in which you define it will change as your life changes. As we grow and learn, and as our lives change, so too do our priorities. Things that seemed important to us in our twenties can often become less significant to us when we hit our fifties. These shifts in no way diminish our ability to become successful. Whatever you do, don't think of a change in how you define success as a setback. Remember that success is the name of the path, not the destination.

6

Your 100-day plan

Remember the rule of the sharpshooter:
You can't hit what you don't aim for

As with all journeys, the journey to success begins with creating forward motion and achieving positive momentum. Not surprisingly, perhaps, the hardest part of this is simply getting started. Once you're partway down a path, it's easier to do the ongoing navigation. But how do you know which path to choose in the first place?

The easiest way to create positive momentum in virtually every aspect of your life is by goal setting; more specifically, by creating and then achieving highly focused short-term goals. One of the most effective models is that employed by many businesses, and popularized by US President Barack Obama: the 100-day plan.

The 100-day plan has become a popular format in organizations, and for good reason. It works. It doesn't seem that long ago that businesses were all-consumed with building three- and five-year plans. Most have come to the realization, however, that the world today changes much too rapidly, and that the things which seem like a good idea today might be absolutely irrelevant three years down the road. While it is still important to have long-term positioning or strategic goals, tactics are best developed in quarterly bursts.

The same is true in our personal lives. Once you've defined success, the next step is a simple, short-term action plan with clearly defined milestones. There are four basic steps:

1. Set a goal.

2. Create a map.

3. Set a timeline.

4. Take action.

Set a goal

Pick something you would like to accomplish that is exciting, meaningful and attainable. Remember that the purpose of these 100 days is to move you a little farther down your pathway to success, so ensure that it aligns with things that are important to you. It doesn't have to be something earth-shattering or momentous, but it does have to be something that will give you a true sense of accomplishment. Here are some examples of 100-day goals we've heard from people in different disciplines:

Salesperson: To have established a solid relationship with five of the ten key players in our target market.

Retailer: To have increased our UPT (units per transaction) by a consistent 30 per cent.

Accounts receivable clerk: To have no customers over 30 days past due.

Executive assistant: To position myself for promotion to Office Manager.

HR Manager: To have a seamless and less labour-intensive onboarding process for all new hires.

Training Manager: To have everyone in the organization skilled in delivering outstanding customer service.

Marketing Director: To have increased consumer awareness of our product by 20 per cent.

In each of these examples, the goals are meaningful (to the individual) and attainable. They are easily measured, and thus easily celebrated. Setting these kinds of goals can have a profoundly positive impact on your motivation. A goal, a target, a *plan* gives you something to work towards.

Create a map

Once you have your goal clearly defined, the next step is to map out the critical elements that have to fall into place for it to be realized, and the order in which they happen. The more time you spend at the beginning of the process, the more likely you will be successful. Ask yourself these two questions: 'What are the things that have to happen in order for me to reach my goal?' and 'In what order do they fall?'

Take, for example, the executive assistant who has set the goal of positioning herself for promotion to office manager. This might be a sample of the sequence of things that have to happen:

1. Learn all of the responsibilities of the office manager.

2. Identify skill sets that need to be developed.

3. Begin developing the skills through courses, videos, books, etc.

4. Assume additional responsibilities that will give her greater relevant experience.

5. Identify the challenges faced by the current office manager, and develop strategies for dealing with them.

6. Communicate to the relevant decision makers her interest in this or similar positions when they become available.

Set a timeline

Take your map, and put dates to each item – up to 100 days. Create milestones – checkpoints – for measuring your progress. If you are a visual person, you can create a timeline, or Gantt chart (Figure 6.1).

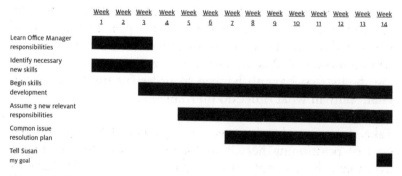

100-day plan: Preparing for Office Manager Position

Figure 6.1

In addition to providing you with a tool for monitoring your progress, this exercise will also help to illuminate how realistic or ambitious your plan is. If you find that you're struggling to put realistic timelines to fit everything within the 100 days, then perhaps your goal isn't realistic. When this happens, try adjusting it by breaking the goal into its sub-components. So, for example, if 'taking over the world' is looking a little ambitious for a 100-day goal, perhaps you should focus on a small country, just to get started.

If you discover that you should be able to achieve your goal in far less than 100 days, then perhaps your target is not quite ambitious enough. Try setting your sights a little higher. A goal that is attained too easily can be just as demotivating as one that cannot be achieved.

Take action

Once your plan is set, the final part is to set the gears in motion. Over the next 100 days, progress from one critical element to another. Stick to your schedule. Mark each day off on your calendar. Don't allow yourself to get off track. To be successful, you have to stay focused – really focused. If something doesn't go as smoothly as it should – turn the burners on and get creative! Have a sense of urgency. You're on a 100-day mission.

If you try this approach, you'll be astounded at how fast the time goes and how much you can actually accomplish. You'll also find yourself energized, and more confident and motivated than ever before. It worked for President Obama, so it ought to work for you.

7

Your winning personal image

*Marketing yourself is no different from marketing anything else –
the product always sells better when it's in a good package*

Why is it that some people seem to get ahead faster than others? How do individuals develop that positive reputation that makes them the 'go-to' people in projects, and gives them the edge in promotion opportunities? I can't count the number of times I've seen two individuals with equal experience, equal skill and equal connections, yet one of them always seems to do just a little better. He gets better treatment, fewer difficult customers, more perks and faster promotions.

A lot of times the unfairness in the workplace that we attribute to favouritism or 'office politics' is really something much less diabolical. Chances are, when you don't seem to get the advantages that others are getting, it's because you aren't *perceived* as deserving them. It could be, for example, that the people around you really just don't realize your workload or the nature of your work. Maybe they're misinterpreting your actions – like perceiving your thoughtful silence in a meeting as disinterest. They may see your well-intended 'devil's advocate' approach to being objective as 'not being a team player'. They may think that because you're off-site a lot you don't do much work. They may not have an understanding of how important your job is to the organization, or the types of challenges you face. It's all about perception, and having access to opportunity is often directly and indirectly a matter of how well you've marketed yourself, and the image you've created.

The most common quality shared by people who get ahead, of course, is quite simply that they are good at what they do. They are competent and reliable, and generally come through when people need them. But the intangible quality, the thing that creates the difference between most of the people who fit this profile and the ones who really excel, is all in their image. It's how they've marketed themselves.

The image you project plays a huge role in how people perceive you. The world's best marketers have known this for years – Nike, Coca-Cola, Wal-Mart, Guinness, just to name a few. They've learned that, as long as you have the substance to back it up, it pays to make sure that everyone knows who you are and what you stand for. They've also proved how very controllable image is.

Some people find the idea of trying to control the personal image we project a distasteful concept. It hints a little of narcissism and shallowness and seems somehow disingenuous. I would argue with this on the premise that, like it or not, image is a reality in all of our lives. People make their judgements of us based on their perceptions of our character. And those perceptions come from the image we project. My point is that, since we're projecting an image anyway, why not try to control it a little?

Marketing yourself does not mean being self-aggrandizing or

self-promoting. Where the latter terms describe boastfulness or selfish actions, marketing yourself refers to packaging and displaying your skills in such a manner as to set yourself apart from others. It's a matter of applying some fundamental marketing techniques. Here are three basic steps to marketing yourself effectively within your organization.

I. Position yourself

Pick one, single quality (not two or three – just one) that you would most like to be known for. It can be anything – honest, trustworthy, humorous, creative, dependable, efficient, efficient, compassionate, competent, confident, action-oriented, meticulous, etc. In marketing terms, it's referred to as a *Unique Selling Proposition or Value Proposition*. Ask yourself, what is the one thing that I bring to the table that makes me valuable to people in my company? Is it your skill, your knowledge, your experience, your network? Pick only one.

Why only one? Why is it important to be so singularly focused? The reality is that if you try to be all things to all people, you ultimately end up being remembered by no one. A great parallel can be found in the world of advertising, where businesses face tremendous challenges trying to stand out amid the shrieking clutter of marketing messages to which consumers are exposed.

David Shenk, in his book Data Smog – *surviving the information glut*, tells us that the average American in 1971 was exposed to 560 advertising messages per day. By 1997 that number had increased to over 3,000 per day. Imagine how staggering that number might seem today. These statistics might seem hard to believe, but when you really think about them, they make alarming sense. How many cars do you pass on the way to work each day, each one sporting at least one logo or nameplate? How many stores do you pass? How many signs do they have on their windows? How many ads are in the daily newspaper you read? How many ads or logos do you see online? The closer you scrutinize our environment, the more you realize just how overloaded our senses are.

Now, to really put this into perspective, try the following exercise. Get a pen and blank piece of paper. In two minutes write down any 10 of those commercial messages you can actually remember seeing today. If you're like most people, you will struggle to recall just five. Five out of 3,000. Scary, isn't it? The point, of course, is that it's hard enough to stand out and be memorable in this day and age. It's impossible if the message you're sending isn't focused.

This lesson is critical as it relates to branding. Here's another exercise: for each of the descriptions below, write down a product name. Don't spend too much time thinking – just write down the first thing that comes to mind:

1. A prestigious brand of car:

2. Fast food:

3. A store with a huge selection:

4. A hotel with impeccable service:

5. Computers that are inexpensive, durable, with great service and available in a lot of stores:

Again, if you are like most people, the answers to the first four came quite quickly, and the last one took considerably longer, if you got one at all. The difference is that the first four are brands that you associate with a single value proposition. The first is quality, the second convenience, the third selection and the fourth service. Our brains easily make the connection between the first four values and the brands because that's how they consistently positioned themselves over the years. The fifth brand we were looking for, however, was one associated with a combination of cost, quality, convenience and service. The value proposition is too complex, and therefore not memorable.

Now think about your work environments, past and present. See if you can put a name of someone who comes quickly to mind for these values:

Thorough:

Hard-working:

Intelligent:

Dependable:

Knowledgeable:

If you were able to think of an individual for any of these values, then that is the way they have been positioned in your mind. They may not have made a conscious effort to do this, but there they are, nonetheless. Branding yourself is the process of positioning yourself in the minds of others, so pick one that works for you.

2. Live it

Now that you've determined your positioning, make a point of reflecting this quality in absolutely everything you do – the way you dress, the things you say, the things you do, etc. Remember that the great brands like BMW, Prada, Starbucks, etc didn't get to where they are overnight. They consistently reinforced their value propositions over and over until they stuck in our collective psyche.

Look for opportunities whenever possible to showcase your

value proposition to the people in your company who are in some way relevant to your career path. Volunteer, join committees, and get involved in projects that highlight your strengths.

3. Be consistent

It takes time and consistency to cultivate an effective image. Don't allow yourself any exceptions. Avoid the temptation to project a different image depending on the person you are speaking with. That approach might give you some short-term benefit, but in the long run it can be devastating.

If you do it right, this process of personal branding shouldn't be all that difficult. Assuming that the value proposition you choose is true to your character, then many of the things you have to do will simply come naturally to you. In fact, if you begin finding this process to be a chore, or you find it difficult to keep the consistency, it's time to re-evaluate what you are trying to accomplish. It very well might be that you are pursuing a value proposition that doesn't come naturally to you.

8

Earning respect

Respect from others is a natural outcome of respect for others

Have you ever noticed that there are some people who seem to have the respect of everyone around them? People hang on their every word, they're trusted implicitly, and everyone turns to them for advice. How does this happen? What have they done to create such an enviable reputation?

Respect in the workplace is something we all seek, yet many people use very counterproductive strategies to try to achieve it. Here are a few examples of how *not* to get the respect of the people around you:

1. Demand it. One of the fastest ways to lose respect from people is to tell them to respect you. While it's true that by exercising position power or threatening formal action, you can force people to defer to you and treat you in a respect-

ful manner, the actual respect they will have for you will virtually disappear.

2. Brag. Some people feel that the best way to get respect from others is to continually tell everyone about their accomplishments. While people might initially be impressed to hear about the wonderful things you've done, it won't be long before they tire of the boasting and label you a braggart.

3. Overcompensate. Some people, in their effort to gain the respect of others, overcompensate by being perfectionists. They pick everything apart. They scrutinize everything to the most miniscule degree. They demand perfection of the people around them, and will point out the smallest and most insignificant flaw in things. This behaviour is remarkably counterproductive, because it really only serves to make people uncomfortable, untrusting and wary of them they're around. The ultimate effect is that it drives people away.

There are some things for which perfection is an absolute necessity. You wouldn't want the air traffic controller at Heathrow, for example, saying to a pilot, 'You're about 500 feet off of the ground, give or take a thousand feet...' Most of our jobs, however, don't need perfection as much as they require *excellence*. The two things shouldn't be confused.

Perfection means that something is completely without flaw, while excellence means to an extraordinarily high standard. People who seek perfection for perfection's sake can become annoying in a hurry. People who seek excellence are respected.

Ultimately, of course, respect is something that can only be earned. This is true whether you want people to respect you for what you do, or for who you are. Here are the three biggest ways to earn people's respect:

I. Be respectful

In the early 2000s, we were working with the senior management team in a government department. One of the individuals – we'll call him Carl – was a professional engineer and a remarkably brilliant man. He also had one of the most unpleasant, arrogant demeanours I've ever encountered.

Carl made no effort to hide his disdain towards his colleagues. When someone made a suggestion he didn't agree with, he would roll his eyes and groan audibly. The result, as you might expect, was that the rest of the group had very little time for him. It was a pity, because intellectually he brought a lot to the table.

Respect is very much reciprocal. The more respectful you are to the people around you, the more they will, in turn, respect you. Be disrespectful, like Carl, and you are guaranteed to have interpersonal struggles.

2. Be good at what you do

When push comes to shove, if you want respect for what you do, you have to be good at what you do. This just makes sense intuitively. Think of the people you respect. Chances are that none of them are just mediocre at their jobs. This is where the concept of continuous improvement that we discussed in the *winning attitude* becomes so important. If you want the respect of those around you, you need to find a niche that you can 'own', and then become an insatiable student. Attend every workshop, seminar and conference you can. Be a voracious reader. Find a mentor. Practise. Become a subject matter expert.

3. Be a 'go-to' person

Be the person that people turn to when they are looking for help. People will respect you when they know they can count on you. Managers in particular love having that go-to person. It is a huge asset for a manager to have someone who just gets things done and doesn't require a lot of hand-holding. When you hear of employees being referred to as 'solid', 'dependable' or as a 'great team player', this is most often what they are talking about. It's a simple thing to do. Just be honest, walk your talk, and make a point of looking out for the people around you.

Having the respect of those around you will play a pivotal role in your success. It's not something that is achieved overnight, of course. It requires patience and persistence and can't be forced, demanded or bought. It is also remarkably fragile, which means that once you have someone's respect you should make sure you don't do anything to compromise that which you have worked so hard to attain. Like a great tree, it can take many years for respect to grow, yet only moments for it to be lost forever.

9

Surround yourself with good people

You'll never see a successful person surrounding himself with mediocrity

Our choice of friends, business associates and our network plays a large role in our success and happiness. These are the people who inspire us, console us, drive us and help us through the tough times. They are also the people by whom we will often be judged. Surrounding yourself with good people is an excellent practice both at work and in your personal life.

Advertising legend David Ogilvy believed that this was one of the principal keys to success. Whenever he appointed a new senior executive in one of their international offices, he would give him or her a set of Russian nested Troika dolls. These are the traditional wooden doll-within-a-doll, within-a-doll, within-a-doll, etc. Typically there are five dolls in all.

As the executive opened the dolls, one at a time, he or she would find wrapped around the smallest doll a hand-written note with the following advice on how to hire people: 'If each of us hires people who are lesser than we are, we shall become a company of dwarfs. But if each of us hires people who are greater than we are, we shall become a company of giants.' That philosophy helped propel him and his companies to the top of the industry.

Successful CEOs are intimately familiar with the importance of surrounding oneself with good people. Watch what happens whenever a new person takes the helm of an organization. The very first thing they will do is create a senior management team of people they know and trust. Many senior executives end up having a virtual entourage – a self-contained team that follows them from job to job. They know how important it is to their own success to have the right people in the right places.

Take a look around your workplace. Who are the people that might be good for your spirit or good for your career? As much as possible, seek people with a winning attitude, values you share, and a genuine interest in others. By the same token, avoid negative people, or people who aren't willing to look beyond their own needs. They can be a devastating drain on your happiness and your future.

Later on in this book, in the winning with people section, we will talk more about networking and how to create connections with the people around you. They are important concepts, and even if you don't aspire to being a corporate leader, a strong network goes a long way to making your job a lot easier and more fulfilling.

10

Action is louder than words

A person's inaction often says as much about them
as their actions

'I should have...'
'I would have...'
'I could have...'
(... but I didn't)

Sound familiar? There are a lot of people out there with a lot of great ideas, and they're quite willing to regale you with the details of what they're 'going to' do. Their to-do lists can be impressive, inspiring and sometimes intimidating. Sadly, though, the vast majority of these 'going tos' end up in the trash heap of 'should haves', 'would haves' and 'could haves'.

When you take a close look at the most successful people around us, you'll find that they aren't always the brightest, strongest, most creative or most talented. They are almost always, however, the ones who choose to take the most action.

'Coulda', 'shoulda', 'woulda' are three things that you rarely hear from the mouths of highly successful people.

The pleasure and pain of procrastination

What holds the rest of us back? What creates the 'all talk, no action', coulda–shoulda–woulda phenomenon? There are a number of things, but perhaps the most insidious is procrastination.

We have all, at some point in time, been guilty of procrastinating. We put things off, delay, ignore, and find myriads of excuses to avoid getting things done. I have a vivid memory of my university paper-writing routine in my dorm room. I would sit there for five minutes, looking at the blank piece of paper until my eyes wandered to some corner of the room. Spying a speck of dust, I would immediately decide that the whole room needed tidying and reorganizing. I had the cleanest room in the residence.

Why do we procrastinate? The experts have identified a number of causes, including perfectionism, unrealistic expectations of how long a task will take, disorganization, feeling overwhelmed, and a fear of failure (or success). The theory I subscribe to is the one best summed up by personal motivation expert Anthony Robbins – that procrastination is driven by the dual forces of pain and pleasure.

Mr Robbins proposes that we are all naturally motivated to seek pleasure and avoid pain. If we have two possible things to do, therefore, and one carries more positive weight on the pain–pleasure scale, we will instinctively migrate towards it. It makes sense when you think about it. The salesperson has a choice of filling out that monthly report or making a call to a client that might increase his commission. The accountant has a choice of returning the call of an unpleasant co-worker or completing the weekly financials. The things we want to do are far more compelling than the things we have to do.

Also playing a role in procrastination is immediacy. The pain of spending 10 hours writing a report today is much more real than the pleasure of having a happy manager in two weeks. Come the night before the report is due, however, we are much more motivated as the pain and pleasure are looming together on the horizon.

The ability to break through the talk and procrastination and actually get things done is the hallmark of all highly successful people. They know that talk isn't really cheap, as the old adage suggests – it's exceptionally expensive. Talking about things without taking action can cost a fortune in time, money and potential. If you find yourself procrastinating, here are six simple strategies that can help get you back on the right track.

1. List the consequences

Make a list of all the negative consequences of putting the task off. See how immediate and concrete you can make the pain that can be associated in putting things off. You'll be surprised at how motivated you can become as the pain/pleasure scale begins to tip. So, for example, if you've been putting off doing that performance review on your team, here's what you might write down:

- I will lose the respect and motivation of my employees.

- I will hurt my relationship with the people in the HR department.

- My boss will make note of it on my review (which might impact my salary and advancement opportunities).

- I may get the reputation as someone who isn't efficient.

When you begin to add it up – loss of employee respect and motivation; soured relationship with peers; negative comments on my record; compromised reputation – all of a sudden the thought of doing those performance reviews doesn't seem so painful in comparison.

2. Set time aside

Structure is one of the most effective weapons against procrastination. When an activity or task is easily slotted into our daily routines, we are less inclined to see not doing it as one of our choices. Here's a simple technique I learned from Manny Rodriguez, an operations manager for a large office complex: whenever you discover that you're procrastinating, write the task you are putting off on a card, and put the card in a box. Set aside one hour each day specifically for doing things you've been putting off. Every day, pull a random card from the box and just do it. This can help give you some structure to things, and miss fewer deadlines.

3. Make a game of it

If you have a competitive nature, you can use this to your advantage. This is particularly useful for those tasks that you don't particularly enjoy but have to do on a regular basis. Set a little mini-goal. Can you do it faster than the last time? Better? Less expensively? Turn it into a challenge.

4. Listen to others

Listen to how often people around you talk about the things they shoulda, coulda or woulda done. Ask them why they haven't done these things yet and then listen to the weak excuses. Sometimes focusing on the behaviour of others can help us better see and correct things in ourselves.

5. Break things down

A lot of times we procrastinate because we feel overwhelmed. There's just too much on our plate and we don't know where to begin. How do you eat an elephant? One bite at a time. When activity starts to bog down, break things down into smaller components and work your way through them one at a time.

6. Put a deadline to everything

Deadlines are motivating – even self-imposed ones. Don't give yourself permission to miss one.

Group procrastination

It's not just individuals who procrastinate, of course. We are also very good at procrastinating in groups. As anyone who has been in the corporate world for any length of time will tell you, one of the greatest productivity killers you can find is meetings.

Have you ever sat in one of those interminably boring meetings where each individual seems intent on speaking just to hear the sound of their own voice? Have you ever been in a meeting where the only thing that was decided was where the next meeting will be? Most commonly, perhaps, have you ever been in a meeting that got so completely sidetracked that absolutely nothing got accomplished? These situations are some of the greatest frustrations people face in today's workplace. Here are a few suggestions on how you can get more out of your meetings:

1. Remove chairs from meeting rooms. The next time you have a meeting, hide all the chairs. You'll be amazed at how much faster a meeting will go when people have to stay standing.

2. Use scrums instead of traditional meetings. Set a time limit for the entire meeting at five minutes. Focus people on the things that need to be said, instead of the things they just feel like saying. It takes a few tries for everyone to get used to them, but once they do, you will find you're accomplishing as much in five minutes as you had been in an hour. People come to meetings better prepared, and are more likely to stay on point.

3. Set a time limit for any discussion. Put a timer in the middle of the table. As soon as it goes off, you have to come to a decision on that point and move on to the next. This ensures succinctness and a sense of urgency.

4. Have an agenda. It's essential that you have an agenda. If you don't, you dramatically increase the possibility of things going off–track.

5. Just start doing it. Instead of waiting for the outcome of a meeting before taking action, go ahead and get started, then announce your progress at the meeting. That old saying, 'better to beg forgiveness than ask permission', is very often good advice. It doesn't always work, of course, but when it does it's a wonderful thing.

One of the great things about this action-first approach is that it helps you to avoid the woulda–coulda–shoulda trap. You've already taken action, and now just have to refine it. You'll discover that this is a common tactic among people who are truly successful in business. You will very rarely hear them telling people what they're 'going to' do. Instead, you'll hear about what they're 'in the middle of', or what they've 'just finished'. They don't talk about their to-dos. They just do things.

Too many people mistake having meetings, striking committees and organizing task forces for taking action. And far too often, we continue these activities long past the point where we should actually be doing something. This is not to suggest that we shouldn't talk about things, or have ideas and plans. But it's not until we actually do something to turn these things into reality that anything is really accomplished. It's an important distinction to make when it comes to your success in the workplace.

The power of patience

We've talked about the importance of getting things done and having a sense of urgency in today's work environment. It seems somewhat incongruous, then, that one of the other hallmarks of successful people is patience.

Our world is moving at dizzying speeds these days. Compared to even just a decade ago, information (and misinformation) now spreads at an impossible rate, and the consequences of our actions can be virtually instantaneous. It's important to recognize, however, that although the things around us are moving quickly, being successful in business and in your personal life is a steady, gradual process.

The best analogy, perhaps, would be that of a farmer. Like the farmer, you plan things out first, plant your seeds, then nurture them and watch them grow. You protect your crop, pull weeds that steal nutrients and chase off creatures looking for a free lunch. You let things grow at their own speed, and wait for the perfect time to begin your harvest. Then, when that time comes, you take fast, decisive action to ensure that you take best advantage of your opportunity.

The analogy works well, because like the farmer, there are many times where trying to rush things will simply lead to frustration and failure. We seek promotions before we are really ready for them. We accept responsibilities we are unprepared for. We take action without understanding the consequences. We take risks with inadequate information. Then when we fail, we lose both momentum and confidence.

In the mid-90s, one of our retail customers had an extremely promising young man working in one of their stores. He had the winning attitude in spades, and was eager to progress through the ranks. By the time he was 25, he had been promoted to store manager, and promptly drove his store to the second-highest sales volume in the chain.

After six months of progressive successes, he approached head office to let them know that he would like to be considered for the position of district manager. In this role, he would have responsibility for a group of a dozen stores. It was hard to argue with his track record, but the company president, Anne, demurred. 'He is a huge asset to our company', I remember her saying to me when I had voiced my surprise at her decision. 'But my instinct is telling me that he doesn't yet have what it takes to manage the business side of a district.'

As it turns out, she was absolutely right. After being told of the president's decision, the young man became frustrated and began looking for greener pastures. He eventually landed a job as a district manager with a national fashion retailer. Six months later he was unemployed.

Despite his intelligence and drive, he had lacked the skill for managing multiple locations and for developing more strategic, long-term approaches to the business. He micro-managed each store manager – so much so that he inadvertently drove two of them to quit. His district floundered, and it seemed the harder he worked, the worse it got.

As you move through your career, keep this in mind. Be ambitious, but don't be too hasty to climb the ladder. Make sure you have all the tools you need – intellectual and emotional – before you make your move to the next level. Remember the importance of continuous improvement, and don't set yourself up for failure. Be a student. Plan your next moves, and patiently stand watch for opportunity. Then, when the door opens, move decisively, firmly and confidently.

There is an old Chinese proverb worth remembering: 'One moment of patience may ward off great disaster. One moment of impatience may ruin a whole life.'

12

The power of focus

Don't be afraid of change. But don't be afraid to leave things alone either

One of the most notable characteristics of very successful people is their ability to stay focused on the things that are important to them, their careers and their business. It's a rare and quite valuable trait. While most of us can stay focused for a limited length of time, we allow distractions and other priorities to gradually throw us off track. Like crows, we become attracted to bright shiny objects, and head off in different directions.

It's no help that so many of today's prominent voices in business continue to proclaim the virtue of *change*. We're constantly being told that new is better. We need to reinvent, reconfigure, change the paradigm, break the unbroken and stay outside the proverbial box. Doing the same thing, or staying focused on the same objectives for any length of time is often considered unimaginative and unproductive. We've become so obsessed with innovation that we've lost sight of the importance of consistency.

Remaining focused on something is difficult because, by definition, it means having the conviction and courage to tune other things out. It means staying the course, leaping the hurdles in front, and passing up possible opportunities that don't lie directly in your path. The payoff to being focused, if you are focused on the right things, can be tremendous. The consequence of not being focused is abject mediocrity.

Timothy Ferriss, in his quirky bestseller *The Four-Hour Work Week*, has a lot of tips on how to weed out the time-killers that impact our focus and ability to get things done. One of my favourite suggestions of his is to reduce your e-mail-checking time to only once a day. His premise is that we are too easily distracted by the constant pinging of our e-mails – often containing unimportant or irrelevant information. His suggestion? Turn the e-mail function off on your computers and PDAs for most of the day. Pick a fixed time, maybe twice a day, to be the time you check and respond to messages. It's a remarkable piece of advice, and it turns out that very few things in our lives are so dramatically time-sensitive that they can't wait a few hours. If you do happen to be in a business where urgent things can happen, he suggests having an auto-responder with your mobile phone number and a message asking people to call you if it is urgent.

Beware the rat race

Lily Tomlin, the iconic US comedienne, once said, 'Even if you win the rat-race, you're still a rat.' It is a sad but accurate commentary. Success in your personal life or in your work life *cannot* come at a price too dear. If it does, then how could you even begin to think of it as success?

Should your approach to achievement be methodical? As much as possible, yes. Should it be thought through, proactive and focused? Yes. But it shouldn't be painful. That just misses the whole point.

The journey of success is like a path through a forest. There are ravines and low-hanging branches that will get in your way. There are creatures that will startle you. There will be forks that require tough decisions. But as long as you're *moving*, and looking at your internal compass to ensure you are heading in the general right direction, take comfort in knowing that your path is as good as any. Take a look around every once in a while to appreciate where you are and how you got there. Enjoy the journey, and the people you meet along the way.

Part 3

Winning in the workplace

> *The best job security in the world comes from continually striving for excellence*

The paths we take on our journey through the workforce today are considerably different from and more complex than those our parents and grandparents took. One of the most profound differences is in the sheer number of jobs we have along the way. The job-for-life mentality that our grandparents had is gone in a big way, with people now averaging between 10 and 11 jobs in their lifetimes. That's 10–11 different workplaces we have to learn to navigate, not to mention all of the peripheral stuff and new learning curves we have to master.

This makes it that much more important, then, that we are skilled and prepared to meet the challenges along the way. This section focuses on some of the core skills and practices that are critical for navigating today's workplaces. It takes the general achievement and success principles from the last section, and provides more specific workplace applications. Not everything applies to every workplace, of course, and each of our professions has unique challenges and hurdles. But with a little effort and lateral thinking on your part, you should be able to take most of the concepts here and apply them successfully in your environment.

As you might expect, your journey to winning in the workplace begins with a *plan*. Where would you like to be in your career two years from now? Five years? Ten years? Most people don't think that far ahead, which is a shame, because without a plan you have very little control over your career path. A common mistake people make is in believing that career planning is only for those seeking powerful, high-level positions. It's not. Even if you're just hoping to maintain the status quo, it's a good idea to know how you're going to achieve it.

With very few exceptions, those people who are very successful in the workplace did not stumble upon that success by accident, by fluke or twists of fate. Nor, as popular folklore might have you believe, do many people attain success by being aggressive or self-serving. The one thing that most successful people do have, however, is a plan. They know what they would like to be doing, figure out how to get there, and then take action. It might not be something as formal as the 100-day plan discussed in Chapter 6, but they have at least given some serious thought to their career paths.

There will be bumps in the road, of course. They are inevitable, and part of the learning process. There may even be times when all seems lost, and your lofty goals suddenly appear quite unattainable. These are your tests, but the good news is that they are open-book tests. Talk to your network and your mentors. Use a lifeline. Call a friend. Remember that it's our own attitudes and perceptions that are often our biggest stumbling blocks. Don't stand in your own way to success.

13

The myths of workplace success

The fastest way to fail is to give up

There are many myths around what it takes to be successful in the workplace, and perhaps before we go any further we should explore some of these. The following are four common ones that can have significant negative impacts on your future if you give them any credence at all:

- the 'look out for number one' myth;

- the 'crazy hours lead to success' myth;

- the 'no time for time management' myth;

- the 'I'm multi-tasking' myth.

Myth #1: Look out for number one

Let's examine two real-life scenarios. The first is about Vic, one of eight salespeople working in a mid-range menswear store. He's been in the store for six years, and, like the others, he works on a straight commission of 8 per cent of his gross sales. Vic knows the game, and how to work it. Although company policy is for salespeople to remain at the front of the store to greet customers as they come in, Vic parks himself in the back of the store where all the suits are. Suits, he knows, are where the biggest sales and biggest commissions are. His philosophy is simple: why greet people at the front of the store when all they might be looking for is a shirt or tie, when I can stay in the back and focus on people who are looking for suits?

His approach, he knows, isn't fair to the other salespeople, and the store manager has spoken to him more than once about it. With everyone else following the rules, Vic sells a disproportionate number of suits. But it's an eat-what-you-kill world, he'll say, and you have to look out for number one.

The second scenario is about Joe. Joe is one of 12 copywriters in a large international advertising agency. Like all of the others on the creative team, Joe knows that television is where the fame and fortune are. The more you have an opportunity to do television, the greater your opportunities and pay grade. Television commercials are also just a lot more fun to do.

The consequence of this (although most agencies won't publicly admit it) is that clients who are involved with other media – newspaper, radio, magazine, billboard, etc – don't have their projects addressed with quite the same degree of passion or expertise. This is a bit of a generalization, of course, but more often than not, the less exciting a project will look in a portfolio, the less attention it gets from the creative team. The impact of this is that agency account managers often struggle to get these smaller projects completed on time and on target. (As one VP once remarked to me, 'Odd, how this creative director can never meet a deadline for the copy for a one-page flyer, but always manages to be on time for a shoot in an exotic location.')

Joe is different. Despite being a senior writer, Joe is always there when people need him for the small stuff. He has fun with it, and presents his concepts for a simple brochure with the same passion as a high-end television commercial. Although he still does his share of television work, he is the go-to guy for the little stuff. It is a stark contrast to the other writers and art directors who quickly duck under their desks when they see a small project coming. Joe understands that the success of the agency depends on everyone pulling their weight.

Fast-forward four years. Where do you suppose they are? If you subscribe to the look-out-for-number-one philosophy, you would think that Vic is prospering and Joe is mired in a dead-end job. That's not how it worked out. Vic is still a commissioned salesperson in the same store, playing the same games, and earning virtually the same income. Over the four years, he has seen three of his co-workers be promoted to management positions (at much higher wages) in other stores within the chain.

In Joe's case, one of the senior account directors he had worked with left for a VP position in another agency. Shortly after, the agency was looking for a new creative director, and he recommended Joe. 'This guy', he told the president, 'has a great creative mind, and is the poster-boy for teamwork.' Joe was hired, and now gets to do lots of television.

The look-out-for-number-one philosophy actually does work. But it all depends on who you define 'number one' to be, and these two stories illustrate it beautifully. If you see number one as being yourself, and you consistently put your own needs ahead of those around you, how many people will you have in your support network? One.

Conversely, if you define number one as being the people around you, and you consistently put their needs ahead of yours, now how many people will you have in your support network? Lots. Which is a better strategy? I'm thinking that the Joes of this world will win every time.

Myth #2: Crazy hours lead to success

There is no question that hard work is a key ingredient to achieving success in the workplace. People who are lazy or take shortcuts rarely excel. The mistake that too many people make, though, is to confuse hard work with excessively long hours. They aren't the same thing. The old adage, 'It's not the hours you put in, but what you put into the hours', is true.

As it turns out, working those crazy hours might actually be *counterproductive* to your success. The returns in productivity begin to diminish after even just a one-hour increase in your workday. Your health, your ability to concentrate, reason, avoid injury and more, all deteriorate significantly as your working hours increase. The impact is measurable. One study of medical residents showed the impairment of working 80 hours a week as being similar to them having blood-alcohol levels of 0.05. (*Neurobehavioural performance of residents after heavy night call vs. after alcohol ingestion*. Arnedt *et al*). A poignant side-note to the study was that not only were the subjects measurably impaired, but they were also largely unaware of their impairment.

The lesson is that, even though we may not recognize it, our effectiveness and general well-being can become compromised if we don't learn to make the distinction between working hard and smart and just working long. It's also worth remembering the tongue-in-cheek 'Parkinson's Law' that states 'Work expands to fit the time allotted.' A lot of times, if there are eight hours to do a job, the job will somehow take us all eight hours to do. But if we suddenly have only four hours to do it, it will magically get done in four hours.

If you realize that you're in a position where you won't be able to complete your workload in the time allotted and you've exhausted all avenues open to you, resist the instinct to simply put in more hours. Take a moment to revisit your approach to work. The first thing you should do is set personal goals for yourself that are achievable. Make sure that you achieve wins every day. Maybe your goal is to have the fewest escalated situations of your team for the day. Maybe it is to ensure that the work you actually do get done is without flaw. Maybe it is to ensure that the critical priorities are all addressed. These things won't help you get all your work done, but they will help keep you positively motivated as you attack the impossible workload.

The second thing you have to do is effectively manage your customers', co-workers' and boss's expectations. Don't tell people you'll get right back to them if you know you can't. Don't promise things you can't deliver. In the most positive way you can, give people a realistic idea of what to expect. They may not be happy with what you have to tell them – but they will at least know that you're trying to do the best you can with what you've got.

Sometimes, yes, you'll still have long grinds and sleepless nights. But working crazy hours for the sake of working crazy hours is ultimately not doing anyone any favours.

Myth #3: No time for time management

As we discussed in Myth 2, a lot of the stress we encounter in our workday comes from a feeling that 'there just aren't enough hours in a day'. Learning new time management techniques is one effective way to reduce this stress, and there are tremendous resources available to help us in that end. There are, unfortunately, a few misconceptions about time management which often discourage people from even looking at these solutions. Here are three of the most common ones.

1. Time management won't help me – I simply have too much work

This is often not the case. Believe it or not, a quick analysis of your current time usage patterns is very likely to show you that you can recover as much as 40 per cent of your workday by simply using your time more effectively. If you're not convinced, try the following simple exercise. For the next week, record your activities in five-minute time blocks. Make sure you write down everything, from the time you spend responding to joke e-mails to the time you spend on every telephone call. If you're like most people, you'll be very surprised to learn where your time is really being spent.

Ana works in the HR department of a large healthcare provider client of ours. She rarely used to answer her telephone when it rang, had large stacks of papers on her desk and always appeared frazzled. When you asked 'how are you?' her answer was always the same: 'Insane. I need a clone.'

On the surface, Ana gave every appearance of someone with far too great a workload. She confided in me at one point that she was at her wits' end and burning out. 'If something doesn't change', she told me, 'I'm going to have to find someplace else to work.'

I had worked with Ana for a number of years, and I suspected that she might benefit from an analysis of her current time usage. Whenever we met in her office, the meetings never ran shorter than two hours – even for mundane things. She would very often stray into non-related areas, and large amounts of personal conversation. Our telephone calls were similar – long and disjointed. My guess was that our interactions were representative of most of her meetings and telephone calls.

The day following our conversation, I e-mailed her a simple log to record her time usage on. 'Thanks, but I don't have time for this', she responded. I suggested that the 15–30 total minutes it would consume in a week might be a good investment if it could save a few hours a week of her time. She agreed, and began recording her time in earnest that day.

After four days had passed she called me. The first words out of her mouth were, 'You knew, didn't you?' Her brief analysis was startling. She estimated that, with all of the non-essential conversation on the telephone alone, she wasted more than two hours a day. She also figured that she could easily reduce her meeting times by over an hour a day. In total, she came up with four hours that she could recover each day.

She then made a few simple changes that had a profound impact on her work life. She bought a small hourglass that timed at about five minutes. Whenever the telephone rang, or whenever she made a call, she would turn it over. When the sand ran out, she ended the call. It took her a while to adjust, but once she had the hang of it, she never looked back. She now sets an alarm on her mobile phone to ring after 30 minutes in meetings, which cues her to try to wrap things up.

Interestingly, the biggest adjustment Ana had to make wasn't sticking to her new regimen; it was dealing with the *result* of it. She was used to working from eight in the morning until six or seven o'clock in the evening, with things still left unfinished. She wasn't used to the feeling of things actually being *done* – much less being done by the official day's end. She felt like she was somehow cheating by going home at four or five like everyone else.

Most of us have never taken the initiative that Ana did and actually analysed our own productivity. Experts agree that we could all stand to benefit from this exercise. It's a pity, because, unlike most other things, time is something that we can never get more of. It's a shame to waste it.

2. All you have to do is organize your time better

While understanding and better organizing your time usage will help, the fact is that sometimes we are just trying to do too much. When this happens, like it or not, something's got to give. Just make sure it's not your sanity. Prioritize so that you're looking after the most urgent and important things first, and delegate as much as you are able. Keep an eye out for time-saving opportunities, but, as we discussed, don't lose sleep over the things you can't control. Understanding what you can't manage is just as important as understanding the things you can.

3. Time management means loss of flexibility

Often, when people hear the term 'time management', they instantly have images of fussy, restrictive systems designed for tightly wound A-type personalities. While it's true that pre-planning, scheduling and creating greater structure to your life can be an effective time-management strategy, it's not the only method. Nor is it the best one for everyone.

Structure of some sort is important to managing your time, certinly, but it doesn't have to be inflexible to be effective. There are a great many effective systems out there and chances are there's at least one to fit your personality type and work style. Do your research. As the example with Ana illustrated earlier, the payoff can be tremendous.

Myth #4: I'm multi-tasking

Multi-tasking has been one of the big buzzwords over the past decade. It's often cited as a key requirement for hiring; and many tools – PDAs being a great example – abound to help us in this goal. There's only one little glitch: multi-tasking, as many people perceive it, is quite literally an impossibility. Like it or not, our brains physically aren't wired to focus on two things at once.

There's a great little exercise that we do in our management training courses that illustrates this very well. We divide the class up into pairs, and give one person in each pair a one-page article on management skills, and the other person a 15-question questionnaire. The instructions are that the person with the article is to read the article aloud while the other person fills out the questionnaire.

When two minutes are up, the people who are taking the questionnaire are asked to recall all they can about the article that was read aloud. Inevitably, one of two things happens. Either they won't get the questionnaire completed because they were concentrating too much on what was being read to them, or they will have the questionnaire completed, but little to no recall of what the other person had said.

Still not convinced? Well, if you're still thinking that people can effectively multi-task, ask yourself this: How would you feel if your surgeon was checking messages on his BlackBerry during your surgery? How would you feel if your accountant was doing your taxes while watching a riveting movie?

Here's the thing about multi-tasking. We can plan and schedule things so that we can have more than one project on the go. And we can jump from one thing to the next and back again very quickly. But we just aren't wired to give more than one thing our attention at any given moment in time. When we try, the inevitable result is that nothing gets done as well or as quickly as it should. Misguided attempts to 'multi-task' have significant implications on our overall success in the workplace. To be successful at something, you have to be good at it. To be good at something, you have to focus on it. Distractions in the guise of 'multi-tasking' impact both the quality and speed with which things get done.

14

Be a champion
of change

Don't wait for something or someone to inspire you.
Focus on being an inspiration to others

If you have any plans at all for career advancement, one thing you certainly have to become comfortable with is change. With as many as 11 different workplaces, you'll be seeing a lot of it before your career is done.

Change, even when it has a positive outcome, is stressful for most people. It creates uncertainty and often challenges our limits as we're forced to embark on new learning curves. It can sometimes be a little overwhelming, and the constant state of flux that seems to permeate the hyper-speed world we live in doesn't help matters. There's so much change these days that a flourishing industry exists just focused on 'change management' – with people telling us how to deal with it, cope with it, manage it, understand it and embrace it.

All workplaces change, and most undergo regular periods of very significant change. Sometimes it's new leadership, sometimes it's a new direction, sometimes the whole organization is transformed by growth, downsizing, mergers or takeovers. In order to truly be successful in the workplace, the best approach isn't trying to figure out how to survive change, however, it's finding ways to *champion* it.

The ability to consistently champion change brings us back to the concepts of perception and choices. Regardless of what the change is, who has introduced it or who it affects, we have to accept that change on its own isn't intrinsically positive or negative, or good or bad. These are just the value judgements we choose to place on it at any given time, based on our own unique vantage point. Unfortunately, as seems to be the case with so many things in life, we are all too often guilty of focusing on the negative. We think about all of the things we might lose in change instead of the things we may gain. We look at the challenges change creates instead of those that it overcomes. We fear the unknown pitfalls instead of anxiously awaiting the unknown benefits.

There are some kinds of change, of course, that we do look forward to. Getting married, buying a new car, having a baby – there are many types of personal change for which we have generally positive associations. But in the workplace we often struggle to find the positives in change.

Your attitude towards change will have a significant impact on how successfully you are moving forward in your career, so it really does make it worthwhile for you to ensure it's a positive one. Henry Chow, a VP Finance with whom I've had the pleasure of working on a number of occasions, has a terrific technique for dealing with the many changes his company has undergone in the past couple of decades. His advice? The next time you're faced with changes in your workplace, make a point of listing all of the positives you can think of that are associated with it. Identify the possibilities that this change may be presenting, and how they might positively impact your career or your life. Once you've done that, Henry will tell you, the secret is not just to wait idly by to see what transpires. Your next step is to do everything in your power to make those things happen.

Henry's story is an interesting testimonial to this. He was working in the financial department of a mid-sized manufacturing company which had just announced a merger with a significantly larger competitor. The term 'merger', as almost everyone in both companies recognized, was just a polite way of saying 'takeover'.

The group Henry worked in was understandably nervous when the merger was announced. The other company had its own, much larger, financial team, and it was widely expected that the smaller group would be expendable. People were scrambling to update their resumés and networks.

Henry enjoyed where he was working, however, and was determined to find a way to stay. He liked the direction things were going in and wanted to be a part of it. So, unlike the others, he sat down and made his list of all the positive things that might come out of all this change.

As he did his research, he discovered that the larger company had two facilities in China, with one, at least, likely to be retooled to provide parts for the smaller company's products. He immediately saw the opportunity. He was intimately familiar with his company's products, and he was fluent in both Mandarin and Cantonese. He sent an e-mail off to the then VP Finance, offering to be a liaison to help ensure that everything was integrated properly.

His proposal was accepted, and he took a lateral position in their Hong Kong office. Two weeks later, virtually everyone else in Henry's group was let go. Three years later, Henry returned to California with a hefty promotion. It was a wonderfully positive life lesson for him. More than once he's reminded me that change isn't an event to be feared, but an opportunity to be seized.

The beautiful thing about all change is that it brings new possibilities and new opportunities. Without change there can be no growth, no improvement, no creativity, no energy. And a workplace without these things quickly becomes stagnant and unfulfilling. Yes, it can be scary. Yes, there are risks. Yes, sometimes unexpected change happens because of unfortunate and unforeseen circumstances. But if you walk through the door of change with your head up, and your eyes and mind open to possibilities, great things can happen.

15

Big picture,
little picture

What you see depends on where you stand

As you move down your career path and transition a few times to different responsibilities, change does become a little easier. Most is obvious – change in location, in responsibility, in hierarchy, in workload. But there are also some subtle changes that take place, almost at a subconscious level, and the more you can become aware of them, the more you can use them to your advantage.

Perhaps the most significant of subtle changes is how very differently you begin to see the workplace as you assume new roles. The effect of this change in perspective can be profound, as it begins to impact your opinions, judgements and actions. Armed with new knowledge and shifted priorities, the decisions and thought processes that seemed so obvious before no longer make the same kind of sense.

This difference in perspective plays a major role in the dynamics of a workplace. When we're working with organizations, for example, we frequently hear people on the front lines make negative comments about decisions made from the top. Comments such as, 'How could they be so stupid?' or 'They just don't get it!' are not uncommon. They see decisions made from higher levels that sometimes appear to them to be arbitrary, short-sighted and sometimes even counterproductive. The negativity that is created can become a significant issue, particularly when a company is undergoing growth or change.

We often attribute these negative attitudes and behaviour to people just being 'resistant to change'. This is very often an unfair assessment. What has typically happened is that the decisions were made with a view to a bigger picture, then just weren't communicated well enough. A lot of times we discover that employee dissatisfaction with management has less to do with the integrity or actions of the management team, and more to do with the employees' inability to see the context from which the decisions were made.

In contrast to this, we've also worked with many senior executives struggling to understand why their programmes and initiatives aren't working. They develop a strategy and action plan that looks great on paper, but fails in the application. They perceive the people charged with executing plans as being lazy, uncommitted, or just resistant to trying new ideas. More often than not, however, when you put these action plans under a microscope, you find that they were developed without adequate attention being paid to the 'little picture'.

Why do these things happen? It's rarely that people are stupid, or lack vision. It's simply a matter of perspective. Our views on the world around us are based on our personal vantage points and experiences. Someone who has never left a life in downtown Manhattan, for instance, would be hard-pressed to comprehend life in the floating villages of Cambodia – just as the Cambodian would have little frame of reference for understanding life in the bright lights and concrete of downtown Manhattan.

Similarly, it's not very realistic to expect a company's CEO to have a grasp on the daily workload of each of their company's employees. Nor, without exposure to all of the factors a CEO must take into account when making decisions, would it be fair to expect a frontline employee to truly grasp the rationale of a CEO's choices. These are the very reasons why clear and free-flowing information throughout an organization is so important to its success.

We once had a vivid opportunity to see this big picture–little picture dichotomy in a large retailer we were working with. We had a training team out in the stores, coaching the employees and managers, and helping them to implement their new skills in a live environment. I was at their head office, working with the senior management team at a strategic level.

At lunch break, I received a call from one of my trainers. He wanted to give me a heads up on some mixed messaging people were getting in the stores. Apparently, he told me, the 'customer first' mentality was not really being championed at the head office. Their store operations team was putting policy before customers' needs, and the store associates were getting frustrated.

The phone call confused me a little. I had just come out of a meeting with the entire senior operations team, and it was the most singularly customer-focused group I may ever have encountered. Yet the source of frustration at store level seemed quite legitimate. After a brief conversation with the VP Operations, though, the cause of the situation became much clearer.

The story unfolded like this: part of the customer service mandate for the sales associates in the stores was to look for ways to enhance customers' experience. Employees were asked to be as proactive as possible in their efforts to create 'Wow!'

customer service moments. In the store our trainer was visiting, the employees had taken this to heart, and had decided to get a little creative.

At the time, the chain was having a 'two for the price of one' sale on a specific line of women's clothing. The people in the store decided to add a hand-written sign below the promotional sign that said, 'or buy one for half-price'. They felt that it provided customers with greater options – something their customers would appreciate. Their logic was that the company still made the same amount of money on each piece, so it was a genuine win–win solution. The district manager had agreed, and approved the sign.

Several days later, however, the regional operations manager for the area found out about this creative thinking, and was incensed. She called the store directly, and ordered them to remove the new sign immediately. She then called the district manager and told her to 'stop second-guessing corporate initiatives' and 'just run the store'. The district manager and the team in the store were frustrated by what they perceived to be a narrow-minded head office person who didn't really buy into the whole 'be proactive and put the customer first' philosophy.

The VP I had spoken with was aware of what had transpired, and told me that, while the manner in which the regional manager responded to the store was not appropriate, her decision was correct. She explained to me that the company had purchased almost four times the quantity of this particular line than it should have. To make matters worse, the new spring fashions were starting to be shown, and this clothing style was not in the mix. They had to move the product as quickly as they could, and were trying to sell as much as possible through their retail locations before they sent the remainders to a liquidator for clearance.

The thought was that, if they could get customers to purchase two at a time, it would help reduce their inventory levels faster.

It was true, the director admitted, that they made just as much money per unit by selling one unit at half price. The only problem was that they would end up selling only half as many.

The marketing tactic was a solid and prudent business move. The issue was created, however, because no one thought to explain the thinking behind the decision to the people in the stores – or at least to the people at the district level. Had they done so, the whole situation could have been averted. The result ended up being two sound decisions – one based on the big picture, and the other based on the little picture, which were completely incompatible with each other.

In the workplace, the more you're willing and able to see a broader perspective on things, the better decisions you will make and the greater success you will ultimately have. It's not easy to do, because most of us become so wrapped up in our own day-to-day roles that it's hard to step back and refocus.

To see both the big and little pictures you need an open mind, and a willingness to constantly question your own views and opinions. You have to postpone placing value judgements on things until you have investigated, asked questions, and listened to the answers. Work on the assumption that the people around you have (from their perspective) sound reasons for the things they do, and then make an effort to understand those reasons. And as you progress up the ranks, try to retain your memories for each level you've worked in. They will help you with your overall perspectives on things.

Being able to see the big picture is critical to anyone's success. A broader scope gives us a better understanding of the implications of our actions, and allows us to look beyond the 'what is' to the 'what could be'. Being able to see the little picture, however, is equally important – because the big picture is only truly understood when we have a grasp of all the little pictures that comprise it. The great people we hear and read about in our lives are often referred to as 'visionaries'. The great failures are often called 'dreamers'. The difference between the two, in many cases, is that the visionaries understand enough of the big and little pictures to actually make the dreams come true.

16

The line (and how not to cross it)

Don't let your words dig a hole that your wit can't get you out of

The ability to connect in the workplace – to engage customers, co-workers, employees and bosses – is more important than ever in our success and enjoyment at work. The closer we get to each other, however, the more critical it is to be aware of the invisible social lines that can create discomfort and awkwardness – sometimes disaster – when crossed: lines between appropriate and inappropriate behaviour; lines between acceptable and unacceptable conversation topics; lines between candid conversation and conversation that becomes too personal.

I have one experience that always comes to mind whenever I think of people crossing social lines. It was in 2001 and a sales rep was trying to sell us booth space for an HR convention in Las Vegas. For the first 30 minutes of our telephone conversation, he was persuasive and personable – so much so, in fact, that I seriously began contemplating purchasing a booth for the show. I began asking a number of questions about the logistics involved, and he answered them all easily.

At one point, after he had answered a question about internet access, I remarked, 'Man, you folks think of everything!' His response to this floored me. 'We aim to please, Shaun', he said, and then his voice took a conspiratorial tone as he added, 'Unless it's my ex-wife, of course. Nothing pleases her. You know what I mean pal?' He then went on a five-minute diatribe about his ex-wife and all of the horrible things she had done to him. I was dumbfounded at what appeared to be an otherwise skilled salesperson getting way too comfortable and crossing well over the line. (Needless to say, I did not take the booth.)

How many times have you seen people make social faux pas that end up alienating them from a group? Sometimes all it takes is a single inadvertent action or word to profoundly change the course of our lives. Here are five general guidelines to help you ensure that you don't accidentally cross any of these lines. They are particularly important when in new environments, or when in the company of people you may not know well.

1. In conversation, wait for other people to introduce topics

This is always a safe practice. If the other person mentions their family, it's usually okay to discuss family. If the other person mentions pets, it's usually okay to talk about pets. Otherwise, stick to the topics that are important to the people around you – even if you don't personally find them terribly interesting.

2. Listen more than you talk

Listen a *lot* more. There's an old Turkish proverb: Listen a hundred times; ponder a thousand times; speak but once. It is great advice on a number of levels. For starters, it's pretty much impossible to learn anything when you're the one doing the talking. Being a good listener also has a marked impact on how you will be perceived in comparison to the talkative people around you. Inevitably, it is the quiet but attentive person who is perceived as more astute.

This isn't new, of course. This same wisdom dates back to biblical times: 'Even a fool, when he holdeth his peace, is counted wise: and he that shutteth his lips is esteemed a man of understanding' (Proverbs 17:28). Despite the seemingly universal acceptance of this wisdom, however, there are an alarming number of people apparently incapable of following it.

3. Focus on facts and avoid your opinions

We all have opinions, but in a new environment it is always safest to keep them to yourself – even when you are asked for them. Indirect answers such as, 'I'm not sure I understand enough about it yet,' or 'There seems to be some validity on both sides of the issue,' are great ways to avoid expressing an opinion that may unknowingly alienate you from others (see Chapter 24 on cold buttons).

4. Avoid alcohol

If you're at a business social function where alcohol is served, never consume more than one drink. I know a young man who had a bright future ahead of him in the real estate business. One unfortunate incident with his boss at the company Christmas party set his career back close to seven years. Never forget that it's a business function, not a frat party. Water is a wonderful thing.

5. Use humour carefully

This is my greatest personal challenge. I love to laugh, and I love to share jokes with people. But more than once I've found myself saying something that someone else thought crossed a line. The best advice comes from a friend of mine in the HR field: Don't tell a joke (or forward a joke e-mail), unless it is material that you would be comfortable sharing with your grandmother.

As a general rule of thumb, when it comes to business inter-actions, always err on the side of caution. It's also important to be aware that these invisible social lines aren't static – they can change depending on the nature of your relationship. And the guidelines that you should follow don't always apply to the people around you. A customer, for example, might launch into a tirade about the wart problem she has on her feet, but this does not mean you should be comfortable reciprocating by tell-ing the customer about your own medical challenges. A boss may confide in you that he or she is having difficulties at home. This does not open the door for you to begin talking about your issues at home.

17

Ten important etiquette tips

*People will remember your actions, for better or worse,
long after your words have faded*

There's a widely held belief that fundamental etiquette in the workplace has been in a steady decline for many years. While many companies have targeted specific inappropriate behaviours such as harassment and abuse, it's hard to argue with the evidence that basic good conduct and protocol continue to slip. It's unfortunate, because regardless of one's position and occupation, the benefits of appropriate decorum are irrefutable. When we scrutinize difficulties encountered in the workplace closely, we discover that many are challenges that we inadvertently create for ourselves, and as such they are quite avoidable. Adherence to some etiquette basics can go a long way to eliminating a lot of stress.

Etiquette is about doing the little things right. It's about positioning yourself as someone who is thoughtful, respectful and caring. It is a broad topic, but to illustrate the types of things you need to be conscious of, I've narrowed it down to 10 little things (in no particular order) that can make a big difference.

Behaviour and workplace etiquette

1. Be punctual

Be on time for meetings and events. Every time you're late, regardless of how good an excuse you have, you send the message, 'I don't care'.

2. Don't use profanity

The use of profanity in the workplace has increased dramatically over the past decade, with some individuals considering it positively *de rigueur*. They think it makes a statement about the kind of person they are. They are most certainly right in that regard.

3. For a good time – ask

If you're walking into someone's office to have a conversation, or if you've called someone on the telephone, it's always a good idea to ask if 'now is a good time'. If the other people are in the middle of something, they may not appreciate your interruption.

4. Respect the people who serve you

We are all judged by our actions. And a great many people subscribe to the common wisdom that you can tell a lot about another person based on how they treat a waiter or waitress in a restaurant. As it turns out, it's a pretty accurate test. With anyone who serves you – inside work and out – make sure that you are always polite and respectful.

E-mail and telephone etiquette

5. Don't write anything you don't want the whole world to see

Be very careful when putting anything into writing. E-mail can be forwarded at the click of a button, and once something gets out into cyberspace, there's no getting it back. It is always a good plan to avoid harsh opinions or judgemental comments in e-mails.

6. Acknowledge every e-mail within four hours

Even if you can't provide senders with the information they need, at least let them know you received their message. You never want someone to feel neglected or unimportant. Sometimes all it takes is a (non-automated) 'Hi Fred. I just wanted you to know that I got your e-mail. I will get back to you as soon as I can with the information you requested.'

7. In difficult situations, respond to an e-mail with a phone call

Telephone or in person is always better than e-mail when dealing with difficult situations. It's amazing how e-mails can go back and forth for days about an issue when one simple little live conversation can usually resolve it.

8. Format e-mails professionally

Forget about your favourite font, background colour, or extra-large font size. In business, the protocol for an e-mail should range from that of a formal business letter to a formal memo. Use Times New Roman or Arial (or similar) fonts in 10-point type. Anything larger comes across as loud, brash and uncomfortable. Don't be concerned with it being big enough for the recipients to read – they can make those adjustments at their end. Make sure everything is spell-checked, and avoid using emoticons or IM short forms.

9. Focus! One thing at a time

When you are speaking with someone on the telephone, resist the temptation to 'multi-task'. Don't be checking your e-mail or PDA in the middle of the conversation. You run the very real risk of missing out on valuable information. More importantly, you don't want your caller to get the message that they are not receiving your full attention.

10. PDA (BlackBerry, iPhone etc) etiquette

There is only one, overriding, all-important rule of the PDA, and it is this:

When you're in a group, a meeting, a workshop, or someone else's office:

TURN IT OFF!

There are far too many people who have become far too comfortable checking and responding to their e-mails and messages in the middle of meetings and conversations. Here's a newsflash – whatever it is, chances are it's not that urgent. Furthermore, it is very unlikely that you are so remarkably important that you have the right to be that profoundly rude. If you absolutely must leave it on for valid reasons, make sure that you inform the host ahead of time.

18

Political correctness

Give the people around you the benefit of the doubt.
Ascribe to them positive motivations, and hope they do the
same for you

When it comes to etiquette and crossing social lines and boundaries, the best illustration has to be the phenomenon most commonly referred to as 'political correctness'. There is perhaps no term which better symbolizes the interpersonal challenges created by the past 30 years of dramatic social change. The heart of the concept has to do with the fundamental, mutual respectfulness which is a prerequisite for a positive and healthy environment. It has become a true touchstone for our words and actions in our personal and business lives – fervently embraced by some, and equally reviled by others.

On the one extreme are the intransigent, the narrow-minded, the bigots and racists who aren't prepared to accept that their actions and views on the world might be antiquated or indefensible. At the other extreme are the hypercritical, activist PC police and 'cubicle cops' who intimidate and bully by stridently and publicly denouncing anyone who crosses their personal sensitivity lines.

Most of us, of course, stand somewhere comfortably in the middle, trying to accept or champion social change as gracefully as we can. Despite our attempts at neutrality, however, it's not unusual to find ourselves occasionally interacting with people at either end of the spectrum. It can be awkward when someone you know or work with crosses a clearly defined line with a joke or comment; or, conversely, when someone overreacts to an innocuous statement or innocent gaffe.

The fact is, for people to function well together, we need to respect each other's needs, dreams, opportunities and abilities. We also must be willing to respect each other's right to their opinions – even those that are very different from ours. The irony is that both the insensitive buffoon and the oversensitive objector are acting in 'politically incorrect' manners. They both represent people who are unwilling to entertain ideas or behaviour that conflicts with their personal beliefs. Although they will be rare, we will inevitably meet people in the workplace who fall into each extreme. The question is, how do we deal with these individuals without alienating them?

Perhaps the most important thing to understand is that, as much as you may like to, there is precious little you can do to change anyone's beliefs or behaviour. Oh, sure, you can scold people, argue with them or correct them, but it's pretty much a guarantee that these actions will likely serve no other purpose than to create even greater tension.

This means that your best strategy, when confronted with extreme behaviour of either type, is that of silent observer. Don't condone. Don't condemn. Don't do anything to encourage the behaviour or prolong the interaction. And if you are asked for your opinion, take a page from the very politicians the term was named after: be noncommittal.

Most importantly perhaps is that, should you by chance catch yourself on a soapbox, lecturing someone about being either insensitive or oversensitive, you may want to look in the mirror, just to make sure the finger is pointed in the right direction.

19

Being a good team player

A team is only effective when everyone is playing the same game

Teamwork is considered to be a critical attribute to most successful workplaces. The better inter-departmental and intra-departmental teams function, the more successful the organization. It's pretty much a straight-line correlation.

This means, then, that your success in the workplace will also be in direct proportion to your ability to function in a team environment. Part of this success, as we've discussed, has to do with a general awareness of the environment – the protocols and culture of the organization. The other part has to do with an understanding of what a team is, and an individual's responsibilities within a team.

The best definition of 'team' I know is: '*A group of individuals working independently and interdependently toward a common goal.*' How do we define a good team player? Over the course of 10 years we asked this question to participants in our team-building programmes. We were able to condense the responses to the following five key characteristics.

1. Focused on the goal

Team players never lose sight of the team's goal. They know what is expected of them, and others can count on them.

2. Aware of others

They are aware of and empathetic to the needs of the others on the team. They appreciate the contributions of others, and understand the interdependency of all team members. Strong team players recognize when a team member requires help, and are proactive to ensure that things continue to go smoothly.

3. Puts the team first

Their decisions are made based on what is best for the team – even when it means personal sacrifices. Other team members know they can depend on them, and never question their priorities or their agendas.

4. Competent

They are good at what they do, and they work hard to ensure that their skill sets are current. They make sure that they don't let the team down.

5. Positive

They are always positive and upbeat. Strong team members will never drag a team down – either literally or figuratively. Even in the most stressful of times, their first response will be 'How can we make this work?' instead of, 'Oh no – this is a problem'.

Pretty simple stuff to be sure, but how well do you fit the criteria? This is one of those areas worthy of some serious introspection. Very few 'poor team players' realize that they are doing things that are limiting their successes, or are aware of the profound negative impact they have on a workplace.

20

Rules for building better workplace relationships

Being nice to people may not always help to get the job done; but it sure makes the process a whole lot more enjoyable

The better our working relationships with the people around us, the better we function within a team, and the better we position ourselves for workplace success. Here are some of the fundamental rules for getting along with people at work that we all need to stay aware of.

Be a rock

Be reliable. Be on time for engagements. Follow through on those things to which you commit. Deliver what you promise. Stand by your friends. Be consistent and loyal. We all like to be around people we can count on.

Lighten up

Don't take things – particularly yourself – so darn seriously. Make the effort to look on the lighter side of life. Learn the art of being genuinely humble. Embrace your own foibles and frailties and learn to laugh at the things that happen around you. Lose the anger.

'If you can't say something nice...'

Most of us have heard the old saying, 'If you can't say something nice about someone, don't say anything at all.' Sound advice, yet for some reason not practised nearly often enough. All too frequently those little comments ('Fred is such a jerk', 'Susan is such a loser', 'Bob is a moron', 'Sally's lazy', etc) will come back to haunt you. You never know when one of those stupid jerk lazy morons is going to hear about what you said. This can really become an issue when you subsequently have to work closely with them – even worse if they end up being your boss.

Equally important is how these statements reflect on you. In many ways, these statements say as much about the person saying them as they do the person being talked about. Every time you say something bad about somebody, you send the message to people that you're negative and judgemental. Talk about people negatively often enough, and eventually it will be you that other people begin talking about.

Don't fall into the trap of being critical of others. The most successful people you'll ever meet in business, and in life, are the ones who give the best of themselves and look for the best in those around them.

Celebrate the success of others

Your co-worker just got a pay rise. Your friend just got a promotion. A former classmate just had a book published. How do you feel about it? The answer to this question will tell you a lot about yourself, and your capacity to connect with others.

To create real bonds with the people around you, you have to have the capacity for true empathy – to genuinely feel their pain and their joy. There is no stronger connection than a shared emotional state. Unfortunately, however, far too many of us struggle with this very basic human concept. Many people, beyond a superficial 'congratulations', can't bring themselves to feel joy for the success of other people. They see life as a competition, with any gain by another as a loss for them. Rather than share the other person's happiness, they feel upset, envious or frustrated. It's an unfortunate and most unproductive emotional state, and if you find yourself falling into this trap, it's time to take a step back and do some serious reflection.

Happiness, as we've discussed, isn't a thing. It's a state of mind. It's a willingness to look for the good that surrounds each of us always. It's finding joy in the positive things you have in your life, rather than dwelling on the things you've lost or don't yet have. Think about it: there are people in this world with little more than a roof over their heads who find a way to enjoy every day. Who is worse off – them, or the people with houses, food, cars and clean water, who live every day spiteful of the things they don't possess?

The next time something good happens to someone at work, make an effort – a real effort – to feel and share the happiness they're feeling. Don't let pettiness and insecurity take over. The result will be positive for you, the other person, and your relationship.

Win with grace

There is a competitive aspect to every work environment. Whether it's trying to win a sales contest, a promotion, the highest ratings, or sometimes even just keep a job, competition is everywhere. And we, by nature, are competitive creatures. Think you're not competitive? Think again. If you really need to prove it to yourself, just ask a friend to hold your head under water for 10 minutes, and you'll see how competitive you become after about the first 40 seconds.

'What about teamwork?' you may ask. After all our discussion about the importance of teamwork it seems a little incongruous now to be promoting our competitive nature. The thing to remember is that operating well within a team doesn't remove competition, it simply redefines it. Let's go back for a moment and look at the definition we gave to 'team': 'A group of individuals working independently and interdependently towards a common goal.' When a team achieves a goal, they succeed. When they don't, they fail. Sounds a lot like competition to me.

Wanting to win is a good thing (assuming that your end goal is not something nefarious), and most people have a lot of respect for competitors. But long-term success is more dependent on *how* you win than it is on just winning. Take, for instance, two sports stars being interviewed after a game. The first goes on a five-minute monologue about how great he is, and all of the great things he did. The second talks for five minutes about how well the team played, and how fortunate he is to be surrounded by such great people. Which one is setting himself up better for long-term success? Which one will get the endorsements, the support of the fans and the support of his team mates? Which one becomes a better role model for youth and has better options to stay in the sport after his playing days are over?

So, whenever you have a win, or whenever you accomplish something, always point your fingers outward to the people and conditions that allowed you to succeed. Don't worry, you'll still get the credit when it counts. Yes, you might desperately want to do your happy dance in front of everyone and shout 'I rule!' but you're really better off doing that when there's no one else around.

Make a difference

One of the exercises we do in our teambuilding programmes revolves around participants identifying people whom they consider to be great role models – people they would be honoured to be compared with. There are always a great variety of names mentioned, often changing depending on the part of the world we are in. Some names consistently come up, regardless of the country we're in, including Oprah Winfrey, Mahatma Ghandi, Nelson Mandela, Bill Gates, Winston Churchill and Martin Luther King, among others. Regardless of who it is, though, when participants are asked to explain their choices, the answer is always the same: it's someone who's made a positive difference in the lives around them.

We value the people in our workplace on a similar basis. The people we respect the most are the ones who make a difference. They get things done, they look after the people around them, they make their mark, they make positive change.

The interesting question is, since we all consistently define people's success based on how much of a difference they've made, why do so many of us who are striving to be successful focus on completely different things? We try to make more money, gain more fame, get more power, etc. Is it really any surprise that so many people who finally achieve wealth, power or fame still end up unhappy?

Do you want to make a difference in the world around you? It's not that hard, really. In fact, you make a difference to the people around you every day, whether you're trying to or not. We've all seen how one individual who comes into work in a bad mood can bring everyone else down; or how one cheerful, positive person can bring everyone up. Each of our actions has a consequence for those around us, as well as for ourselves. The secret, though, is to do it consciously, and try to ensure it is a positive difference we're making, not a negative one.

Just before you begin the next section of this book, make a commitment to yourself to make a positive difference in the life of someone else over the next month, whether it's donating an hour of your time to a charitable organization, giving some money to a worthy cause or simply giving a warm smile to someone that needs cheering up. Each of these makes the little piece of the world around you a better and happier place to be. Make it your mission to make your mark, however humble. The road to greatness often starts with just one simple random act of kindness.

Part 4

Winning with people

Every day brings the opportunity to make a difference in someone's life

Over the past couple of decades, technology has taken the absolute forefront in shaping our societies. Communications technology and computer technology (cellular telephones, e-mail, the internet, etc) have forever altered the way in which we conduct business and live our lives. The exciting end result is that we can now more easily and effectively connect to each other than any of us could possibly have imagined.

Unfortunately, however, our lives have also changed in other ways. Stress and conflict in the workplace have soared in the past 20 years. Customer behaviour seems to be getting worse with each passing day. Fundamental etiquette, and what used to be called 'common courtesy', is changing from being the norm to being quaint and idealistic. Somehow, somewhere along the line, as we were learning how to connect *to* each other, we started forgetting how to connect *with* each other.

The one immutable secret to connecting with people

So what is the secret to connecting with people? What is the element that seems to be eluding us? What is it that companies are missing in their efforts to provide world-class customer service, and managers are missing in their efforts to build a loyal, motivated workforce? The answer is as simple as it is elegant. It's the timeless rule of getting along with people we were taught as children:

**The more you care about the people around you,
the stronger your relationships will be.**

Think about it. Think about the last time you, as a customer, had an unpleasant experience with a company. What was the overriding message you got from the company that made the experience so unpleasant? It was that you, the customer, didn't matter. They didn't care about you. What is the number one complaint that employees have of bad bosses? It's that their bosses treat them as though they are unimportant. What is the number one complaint that bosses have of unpleasant employees? It's the sense that these employees don't care about them, the company or their co-workers. After 20 years of researching customer service, leadership, teamwork and conflict management, I can state unequivocally that your ability to connect with another human being is directly proportional to the degree to which that person thinks you care about them.

So what does this mean? Well, for starters it means that, if you want to work with people, you have to like people. Pretending isn't good enough. You actually have to really care about the people around you. You have to want them to be happy, and you have to be prepared occasionally to put their needs ahead of yours.

For companies that want better customer relations and better customer loyalty, it means that every aspect of the company has to send the consistent message, 'we care about you' and 'you're important to me'. It means that the time has come to stop dehumanizing customers' experiences. Cute automated telephone systems, for example, that try to mimic a human experience only reinforce the message that you're too big to actually care about your customers one-on-one. Customers want to deal with competent, confident, compassionate and cheerful people who are empowered to do the right things – not machines that have none of these qualities.

You want to build greater employee loyalty? Send them the same message. Let them know in your words and actions that they are important to you and that you appreciate their efforts. The same rules hold true for individuals who are looking to create more positive relationships, build stronger networks, generate greater sales, or improve the workplace environment. There are veritable mountains of research telling us that people everywhere – customers, co-workers, employees and employers – just want to be associated with people and businesses that care about them.

This section deals with the best ways to send this simple message effectively and consistently. In it, we will also explore those things we do which all too often send conflicting messages and limit our chances to connect with the people around us. It's an important section – arguably the most important – because unless you work deep, deep in a mine somewhere, you always have to deal with people.

21

First impressions

Why leave people's perceptions of you to chance?

Our ability to connect with the people around us begins with the very first moments of our very first encounter. The old sayings, 'You never have a second chance to make a first impression' and 'First impressions are lasting impressions', are more than just popular folklore. There is a tremendous amount of research to indicate that all it can take is a single, brief encounter for people to form a virtually unshakeable opinion of you. It's actually a little unnerving sometimes to think of the long-term impact a single encounter can have on how you are perceived. In fact, as illustrated in a 1980 study by Nisbett and Ross, people's first impressions of you will continue to stick, even when later evidence overwhelmingly tells them that they are mistaken.

So, what does it take to create that positive first impression? The words we choose, our demeanour, our voice tone, all play a role. People often begin to form an impression of us even before we get a chance to open our mouths. Long before we start speaking, their eyes are sending messages to their brains for processing.

Five rules for making good first impressions

Here are five critical things to remember to ensure you make a good first impression with the people you meet.

1. Smile!

You've heard it a million times, and it's worth repeating once again. There is nothing that sends a positive message to another person faster than a warm, genuine smile. People can even hear a smile over the telephone.

Before you just brush this off as motherhood advice, do this little experiment. Take a day – a full day – and just watch people interacting. Go shopping. Watch clerks and salespeople interact with their customers. Watch co-workers in your business talk to one another. How many do you suppose will be smiling? Unless you live in the magical fantasyland of Happyville, the percentage will be frightfully low. And unless you are truly an exception, the people you observed aren't much different from you.

'So what?' you might ask. 'Does smiling really make that much of a difference?' Fair question. We do this little exercise in our customer service training that serves as a poignant illustration of why smiling is important. We bring people up to the front of the room one at a time, and show them a flash card. The flash card has an emotional state printed on it – Happy, Sad, Mean, Angry, Confident, Assertive, etc. People are instructed to stand with their hands behind their back, and try to get that emotion on their face. The rest of the group then shouts out what they think the person is trying to communicate.

The exercise is as painful as it is persuasive. The first flash card that we show is *Happy*, and the entire group gets it in an instant, and shouts it out in unison. After that, it's a crap shoot. Sometimes the trainer actually has to prompt the audience by giving them the first letter, then the second, and so forth. Words that we would normally associate with positive things, like Confident, Relaxed, Assertive, Thoughtful, get the most frightful responses from the audience. *'Ticked-off!'* *'Cold!'* *'Arrogant!'* *'Depressed!'* *'Lazy!'* *'Constipated!'* all reverberate around the room. The real kicker comes at the end. The last person to come up gets a flash card that says 'No Expression', and, like before, the results are never good.

There are two points that the exercise illustrates. The first is that there is only one facial expression that can't be misunderstood, and that is a smile. All of the other expressions are open to wide interpretation, and those interpretations are rarely *more* positive than intended. The second point is that our faces, when we think they are expressionless, are actually sending clear messages that are counterproductive to us connecting with other people.

The impact of a smile can't be overstated. If you're still sceptical, however, try this next exercise: tomorrow, spend the entire day as expressionless as you can. Resist the temptation to smile, or even raise an eyebrow. On the following day, smile at everyone – not a 'Hey, I just got some new medication' kind of smile, but a genuine, warm smile. You have my absolute guarantee that you will see a profound and positive difference in how people treat you from one day to the next.

As it relates to first impressions, the speed with which people form judgements based on our facial features is astounding. A study by Janine Willis and Alexander Todorov at Princeton University identified that we will draw trait inferences after just a 100-millisecond exposure to a facial expression. *That's 1/10th of one second!* The fascinating thing about this study is that these judgements formed in a split-second do not change significantly over time. That's a powerful argument for keeping a smile on your face.

2. Make eye contact

Unlike the idea of smiling, you've probably only heard this one half-a-million times, and it, as well, is critical to ensuring a positive first impression. Most of us are aware of the importance of eye contact in making connections with the people around us, and yet for some reason most of us don't really do it nearly as often as we should. The degree to which you make eye contact with people plays a huge role in how you are perceived. It conveys confidence and interest, and lets the other person know that you are engaged in the conversation. Avoidance of eye contact also sends messages – bad ones. If you fail to make eye contact, people can perceive you as unsure, disengaged or even dishonest.

Good eye contact isn't a 'who blinks first' contest, of course. You don't want to overdo it and unnerve people. But during a conversation it should be frequent, and the duration should be a full three seconds each time. Don't just look at someone's eyes – look into them. Make a connection. Let them know that, for this instant, they are the most important people in your life.

Here's another exercise for you: the next time you're walking down the street, try to make eye contact with everyone you pass. It's a great study in human nature. Chances are, the majority of people will either not see you, or will glance at you and then quickly glance away. Those who do maintain eye contact with you will very often smile at you as they pass. You'll feel the connection.

Your skill in using eye contact is a remarkably powerful tool in building both business and personal relationships. Practise with the people around you. See for yourself the difference it makes in how others respond to you. You may be quite pleasantly surprised at the results.

3. The handshake

There is perhaps no single action in the business world that creates a connection with people faster than a handshake. A proper handshake conveys confidence, warmth and charisma. A poor handshake can send the message that you are unprofessional, disinterested and socially unskilled. The mechanics of a proper handshake used to be a given – a fundamental social skill that really didn't warrant much discussion. Most business professionals I speak with nowadays, however, agree that fewer and fewer people seem to understand how to shake hands well.

So, for the record, here are the dos and don'ts of a good handshake:

- **The perfect handshake:** It begins with lots of eye contact and a brief, warm smile. Extend your arm with your hand perpendicular (thumb to the ceiling), neither dominant (palm down) nor submissive (palm up). Move your hand firmly into the other person's until the web between your thumb and forefinger are making solid contact with theirs. Firmly close your hand over the other person's hand for 1–2 seconds with the same grip you might have when holding a heavy frying pan. Make a subtle, almost imperceptible up-down motion, then release the other's hand. Remember to keep your fingers together.

- **Handshake don'ts:**

  1. Don't crush the other person's hand. You're connecting, not competing.

2. Don't keep your hand limp. The 'dead fish' handshake says 'dead fish personality'.

3. Don't do the 'finger squeeze'. This is a common style where you just bend your fingers over the other person's. It comes across as unprofessional, and just feels icky.

4. Don't pull away. If you briefly touch the other person's hand and pull away, the other person will feel rejected.

5. Don't splay your fingers. Somebody, somewhere began teaching women that, because of having smaller hands, they should splay their fingers out slightly to make their hands seem larger. That's just really bad advice. Like the finger squeeze, it just feels unnatural to the other person.

The same rules for handshakes apply for both men and women. It's a fairly simple gesture, but it's critical that you learn to do it well. If you are unsure of your handshake, practise with a friend or family member. It's much too important to leave it to chance.

4. Be interested

When you first meet someone, one thing you really want to resist is the temptation to talk about yourself and the things that interest you. This is actually good advice at any time, but particularly important when it comes to creating a first impression. Make a point instead of learning about the things that interest the other person and of demonstrating an interest in the things that interest him or her. It's amazing how quickly you can establish a positive bond when you create mutual interest.

5. Walk on the lighter side

We mentioned the importance of lightening up in the last chapter, and nowhere is it more important than in creating that first impression. Perhaps the single most effective way to create a positive first impression or establish a connection with people is through humour. Humour can break the ice in an initial meeting, take the edge out of conflict, reduce the stress when things go wrong and put people at ease. We typically appreciate the individual who can lighten the tone of a situation with a few well-placed words. To be that person, you don't have to be a stand-up comedian or have a repertoire of witty jokes. In fact, you don't really even have to be funny. All you really need is the willingness to look on the lighter side of things. If you can make the effort during stressful times to find something that will make people forget about their stress – even for a moment – you become a valuable commodity indeed.

There are some people out there who are pretty intense – taking things, and themselves, way too seriously. And while their passion and focus are admirable, they're hard to be around for much more than brief intervals – particularly during stressful situations. One thing's for sure, you don't want to be that person. Not if you have any aspirations of being successful with the people around you.

When you get bent out of shape over little things, not only do you raise your blood pressure, but you raise the blood pressure of the people around you as well. People see it as selfish behaviour – and rightly so. Make it your mission to try to make those around you as comfortable as possible, and they will truly appreciate it. Making the effort to look on the lighter side of things goes a long way in accomplishing this.

When you're hot, you're hot

One of the very compelling side-effects of creating a positive first impression has to do with the halo-effect that it creates. Once your positive first impression is set, it becomes a solid foundation for how people will perceive you in the future. This phenomenon was highlighted in a 1988 study conducted by Widmeyer and Loy.

In their study, they had a person posing as a university professor give a 'neutral' lecture to a large class of students. Half of the students had been informed ahead of time that the professor was a generally warm person, and the other half were told that he was a generally cold person. When polled afterwards, the students who had been told the 'professor' was a warm person rated him as significantly more effective, less unpleasant, more humorous and less ruthless than those who were led to believe he was a cold person. What this suggests is that, if you're able to create a positive impression at the beginning, you'll get a lot more mulligans for subsequent faux pas and slip-ups.

Once you've established a positive first impression, the foundation for a business relationship has been set. The key, after that, is twofold: 1) to consistently demonstrate a few very basic interpersonal qualities; and 2) to avoid stepping on social landmines. These are the things we'll be covering over the next few chapters.

22

Outward focus

Look after your friends, or soon you won't have any

Charisma factor

As part of our research into what comprised a winning attitude, we isolated 35 individuals in the original group of 86 who had been defined as 'charismatic'. It's fairly obvious that charismatic people have an edge in organizations, but the definition of charisma has always been somewhat vague. The Merriam-Webster Dictionary, for example, defines it as 'a special magnetic charm or appeal'. An accurate description, no doubt, but not very instructive for someone seeking to develop this quality. We wanted to find out what, if any, characteristics these people had in common.

The first thing we had to account for was the 'charisma by position' factor. People in more senior roles in an organization will naturally have somewhat of a gravitational force due just to the organizational or position power they wield. A corporate CEO, regardless of how dry and uninspiring, will still have more people following him than an equally dry and uninspiring person in the mailroom. The question, of course, is, are people charismatic because of their position power, or did they reach their positions in part because of their charisma? While there is most certainly truth to both arguments, the evidence points more to the latter. It makes more sense to believe that Tony Blair or Barack Obama, for example, already had a great deal of charisma prior to reaching the pinnacle of their careers, than to believe that they suddenly developed charisma at the end of an election.

Our test group supported this. Interviews with friends and co-workers of the people in the test group confirmed that charisma was a characteristic of these people long before they had achieved any sort of position power. Armed with this reassurance, we were then comfortable in the assumption that it wasn't the position these people held, but instead *what they were doing* that created the perception of charisma. When all the data dust had settled, we had determined that our test group had four very common characteristics. We labelled them Confidence, Positive Attitude, Positive Demeanour and Outward Focus.

The first two, Confidence and Positive Attitude, are the internal characteristics, and components of the winning attitude that we reviewed in the first section of this book. The third characteristic is Positive Demeanour. It is the outward manifestation of a positive attitude – adherence to fundamental etiquette and protocols that we addressed in the winning in the workplace section. The fourth characteristic is Outward Focus, and it may be the most rare and valuable of the four. An outward focus, defined simply, is placing the needs of other people at a higher priority than our own. A classic example is the story of Sir Walter Raleigh who reputedly removed his cloak and threw it over a puddle so that Queen Elizabeth wouldn't get her shoes dirty as she walked from the street to the kerb.

The fact of the matter is that we all value, respect and honour selfless people. But such individuals are tough to find. Self-lessness comes at a price too dear for most of us. It means giving of yourself, giving some more and giving again, with no promise, explicit or implied, of a return. That philosophy is rare indeed in our modern quid-pro-quo society, where today's equivalent of the gallant Sir Walter Raleigh would be more likely to turn to the Queen and present her with a dry-cleaning bill.

Perhaps the best illustrations of outward focus come in the area of customer service. Not surprisingly, the most highly skilled service providers you'll meet are also quite charismatic by nature. When I collect stories of outstanding customer service, outward focus is a theme that recurs over and over again. I hear about the young store clerk who works 30 minutes after closing time on a Saturday night to help a desperate customer. I hear about a graphic designer working 48 hours straight over a weekend to help out a panic-stricken customer. I hear about a city bus driver sprinting into a shop to retrieve a purse left in a store by a blind passenger.

If we take customer service to a macro level, beyond the business world, we hear about our firefighters – facing possible injury or death, racing *into* a burning building because someone in there, someone they've never met before, needs them. These levels of commitment – of absolute selflessness – are the things we all admire and respect in others. They are things we want in those who serve us. Yet precious few of us expect it of ourselves.

The importance of an outward focus on your success in dealing with people can't be overstated. As any professional speaker, trainer, actor or comedian will tell you, in order to be successful when you're on stage, you have to be prepared to do whatever it takes to connect with the audience. Your needs, your feelings become unimportant as you work to influence the audience's emotions. You live the moment for them – not for yourself.

Your payback comes at the end – if you were good – when the audience rises to their feet in thunderous applause.

Most people profess to believe in the philosophy of 'what goes around comes around' – in karma – but when push really comes to shove, most of us still don't quite trust it. The greatest difficulty most of us have is getting past that quid-pro-quo mentality. Most of us are prepared to deliver the pro quo, but only after we have assurances of the quid. But karma doesn't work that way. Neither does an outward focus. An outward focus is about focusing on another person, knowing that you may never see a payback from him, but trusting that payback will come in some way at some time.

Should you look out for number one? As we discussed in Chapter 13, it all depends on who you define number one to be. Read the stories of anyone who has achieved greatness, or of anyone who professes to be genuinely happy and successful in their lives, and they'll tell you that they ultimately got what they wanted by first ensuring that those around them got what they needed. That's what outward focus is all about.

23

Two big hot buttons

Don't just stop and smell the roses;
plant a few for other people to enjoy

Sometimes we forget just how much influence we have over the actions and attitudes of the people around us. Beyond having the right attitude and a strong, outward focus, it requires an understanding of how to push the right buttons in the right people at the right time. Hot buttons are things that positively alter someone's state: words, phrases, actions or activities that create a positive change in someone's behaviour or attitude. We'll be talking about how best to manage our choice of words a little later on in this section, but I want first to go over two absolute must-dos when it comes to connecting with people.

1. Listen

Listening has come up a few times already in this book. It is a skill that permeates every aspect of success, and most of us have heard of the importance of listening many times since we were very young. Despite the constant reminders, however, few people really develop their listening skills much beyond mediocre. How good are your listening skills? Take this simple test:

a. Has someone ever said to you, 'I just said that'?

b. Have you ever found your thoughts drifting when someone else is speaking?

c. Have you ever been introduced to people, only to forget their names a minute later?

d. Do you check your e-mails while talking to people on the telephone?

e. Do you sometimes find yourself thinking about your response when another person is speaking?

Chances are you answered 'yes' to at least one of these (or, if you're like most people, you answered yes to all of them). Welcome to the world of the average listener.

Is improving your listening skills important? Regardless of what you do, the answer is a resounding yes. Better listeners make better bosses, more valuable employees, more effective service providers, higher-producing salespeople, better parents – the list goes on. Listening is, in many ways, as much an art as it is a science, and to be good at it you must be both involved and interested.

The great thing about being a good listener is that almost everyone, when given a chance, enjoys the opportunity to talk – particularly about themselves – their children, their pets, their accomplishments, etc. This increases the value of a good listener dramatically. The more you listen, the stronger your connection becomes with someone. There are two compelling reasons for listening to others' stories.

People like you more

When someone is talking about himself, and you are listening intently, you send the message that the two of you have at least one interest in common – him. What would there be to not like about you?!

People respect you more

In the early 1990s a business associate and I met with a company marketing director who had inquired about our customer service training services. After the initial introductions, she began talking about all of her achievements in the company. For close to 40 minutes, we listened, and she talked. And talked. And talked. By the end of the monologue, she had told us what we were going to do, when we were going to start, and how much she was going to pay us. The only sentence that either of us got in was at the very end, as we were leaving. 'Would you like us to send you some information about our company?' I inquired.

'No', she said with finality. 'From our conversation today, I've learned everything I need to know. I like the way you do business, and you obviously know what you're doing. The job is yours.' We were dumbfounded. We had quite literally said nothing during the time we were there, yet she was completely convinced of our ability to deliver to her expectations. I learnt that day the power of listening.

Work on your listening skills. Practise them. The payoff is huge. Good listeners are scarce, and very much in demand.

2. Praise

There is a lot of very compelling research about how positively people respond to praise. Flattery, when it's not 'over the top', is an extraordinarily powerful way to influence someone's behaviour. A 2004 Gallup survey of over 10,000 business units in 30 industries found that regular recognition and praise has significant, wide-ranging impacts on people. Some of the benefits they cited include increased productivity, increased loyalty, more positive co-worker interactions and better customer service experiences.

It's a principle that you can easily test yourself. Pick someone today – anyone – and say something nice about them (make sure that the compliment is genuine). Then sit back and watch how their mood and behaviour change. It's a remarkable phenomenon.

Whether it is in the workplace or in our personal lives, we all appreciate praise and recognition. A kind word from a friend or co-worker can make your day – and also makes you look at the person doing the praising in a more positive light. The practice is valuable in every aspect of your life. Verbally recognizing our children's accomplishments gives them confidence. Telling employees how good a job they've done motivates them to do it again. Acknowledging a friend's success reinforces your relationship. Letting co-workers know how much you appreciate their efforts strengthens a team. The list is endless.

Given how truly powerful praise is, the real surprise is how rarely we hear it. A lot of times, we assume that people don't want to hear it, or that it's unnecessary. Sometimes, tragically, we fear that people may judge us as being insincere. But most often we are simply so caught up with our own issues that we don't even notice the small successes and accomplishments of those around us.

Genuine praise is a powerful way to strengthen relationships. To be effective, there is one key rule to follow – praise the specific action, not the person. It is a subtle difference, but a very important one. For example, instead of saying, 'Susan, you are incredibly smart', say 'Susan, that was an incredibly smart decision.' What's the difference? The first one is a value judgement about Susan herself. The second is a comment on her action. Susan will be likely to agree that her decision is a smart one, and therefore accept praise about it. But it is very possible (and more common than you might think) that Susan does not see herself as a smart person. If this is the case, she will be less likely to give credibility or sincerity to your comment.

These two hot buttons, listening and genuine praise, are exceptionally powerful indeed, and it is hard to imagine how they could be over-used. Don't be shy about practising and applying them as much as you can.

They aren't the only hot buttons, of course. There are as many different hot buttons as there are people out there, and the better you understand them, the better relationships you'll be able to forge. To learn someone's unique set of hot buttons, all you have to do is observe them. Look for things they are passionate about – the things that make them laugh, the things that fire them up, etc. While you're at it, see if you can't figure out what your own hot buttons are. You never know when one might come in handy for a little self-motivation.

24

Cold buttons

*What we say and what other people hear are
rarely the same thing*

You'd think that building relationships with people – either
personal relationships or business relationships – should be
easy for us. After all, as any anthropologist will tell you, humans
are social creatures by nature. It's natural for us to interact with
others. It's natural for us to build relationships and form social
groups. So why is it that we so often struggle in our efforts to
connect with the people around us? Sure, we can blame stress,
circumstances, outside factors, karma – any number of things.
But the truth is, a lot of our social challenges are often self-
inflicted. And most of them are entirely preventable.

Along with hot buttons, we are also all fully equipped with our
own unique set of cold buttons. We all have words, phrases and
actions that get our dander up a little when we are exposed to
them. Have you ever been in conversation with someone, and

suddenly noticed that they no longer seem engaged? Have you ever had an interaction with a customer or co-worker that inexplicably went sideways? There's a good chance that you accidentally triggered the response by tripping over one of their cold buttons.

Where hot buttons send the message that you are interested in the other person, cold buttons typically send the message, 'I don't care'. Here are some common cold buttons that you should really try to avoid pushing if you want to get along with the people around you.

One-upmanship

Don't feel compelled always to have a 'better' story or experience than the other person. Don't even try to match it. When you do this, you trivialize what the other person has said. Listen appreciatively to what the other person is saying. Nod, smile and laugh when appropriate then shut up.

Remaining expressionless

Remember the discussion on how quickly people make judgements about us based just on our facial expressions. When you don't make an effort to be responsive to others through your face and body language, you send the message to people that they are unimportant. Smile, for goodness sake!

Correcting people

Some people live to be contrarians. It doesn't matter what you say, the first words out of their mouths are '*Yabut (Yeah, but)*...' or '*Although*...' Unless it's truly important, don't correct things other people say. It just sends the message to them that you think they're stupid.

Lack of interest

Want to connect with other people? Be interested in other people. Genuinely interested. No one wants to connect with someone who is only interested in himself.

Lack of effort

Building any relationship takes effort. Don't sit at home waiting for the phone to ring – call someone. Don't wait for your boss to tell you why she's not happy – ask her. Don't wait for your employee to threaten to resign before you talk to him – talk to him now. Don't wonder what it is that your customers are looking for – find out.

Lack of humour

A lot of us take ourselves way too seriously. As we discussed earlier in the book, you don't have to be a stand-up comedian to connect with people, but no one likes to be around someone who's always intense. If you're not finding a reason to laugh out loud most days, you're probably not a lot of fun to be around.

Being opinionated

Opinions are an interesting topic, and warrant some discussion. Sometimes opinions are based on facts, sometimes on experience, sometimes on misinformation, and sometimes they're based on nothing at all. Opinions are everywhere and we all have them. Curiously, while people are often hesitant to share other things they have (chocolate and money as examples), opinions always seem to be there for the taking.

The fascinating thing about opinions is that, unlike facts, their value does not increase or decrease based on their accuracy, relevance or timeliness. Rather, the value of an opinion is mostly dependent simply on whether or not it has been requested. We will generally value someone's opinion when we've asked for it, but an uninvited opinion rarely holds the same value to the recipient – even when the opinion is 100 per cent accurate.

One of the greatest secrets to connecting with people and building strong relationships is knowing when to share your opinions, and knowing when to keep them to yourself. Chances are you've seen at least one relationship become weakened, either business or personal, because of an inappropriate or untimely point of view being presented. And most of us know at least one person who seems completely unable to resist telling everyone around what he or she thinks.

Here's the thing: sure you're smart – but that doesn't have to mean everyone else is a moron. If other people ask for your opinion or knowledge, then by all means share it. If they don't, keep your thoughts to yourself. The irony with opinionated people is that their very opinionated behaviour often causes other people to begin forming opinions about them.

Hopefully, you've recognized most of these common cold buttons. You may even have recognized one or two of them that you've inadvertently pushed at some point in time. They are social landmines that are quite worth avoiding. It's hard enough as it is to build strong, positive relationships with people at work without having to repair rifts caused by preventable social gaffes, so be careful.

25

The way of words

If there's more than one way to say something,
why would you not choose the better way?

A good friend of mine, Brian, headed off one Sunday afternoon to use the driving range at a local golf club. To his shock, he was turned away. The reason, the young lady behind the counter told him, was because the range was only for the use of people who were golfing on the course that day. The next day he called the course and asked to speak with the manager. He explained to her that he had used the range many times over the last five or six years, and this was the first time he had ever heard of this rule. The manager's response floored him. 'Well', she said to him, 'I guess you've just been getting away with it all these years.'

Getting away with it.

Although she very likely didn't intend it in this way, her words suggested that Brian had knowingly been doing something wrong. Needless to say, the implication didn't sit well with him, and neither he nor his friends have golfed at that course since.

Your choice of words plays a profound role in how well you connect with other people. It can be the difference between conflict and comfort, connection or rejection, making a sale or losing a sale, a promotion or stagnation. Your language skills communicate messages about your attitude, your education and your personality. The right choice of words can open a myriad of doors for you. Saying things the wrong way, however, can sometimes have the exact opposite effect you were hoping for.

Learning to use language skilfully is more than just watching what you say, or trying to walk that often overzealous line of political correctness. When used well, words can motivate, stimulate, educate, persuade, influence and set a tone. It's a subtle, yet extraordinarily powerful skill. It's the difference, for example, between saying, 'I think that was a stupid thing for you to do', and 'I'm not sure that's the way I would have done it'. The first one is accusatory and demeaning, the second one gentle and less confrontational.

Here's a great practice: listen carefully to the words that people around you choose. And the next time someone says something that gets under your skin, ask yourself, 'How could this person have conveyed the same message in a way that wouldn't have bothered me?' Being aware of the language strategies other people use can significantly help you improve your own communication skills. It's truly amazing the difference just a few well-selected words can make.

The following are five great language tips that we should all have in our toolbox.

1. 'Excellent', 'Outstanding', 'Brilliant'

Rather than just saying 'Thank you' the next time someone does something for you or gives you something, try saying 'Excellent, thank you!' and watch how positively the person responds. It's almost magical the way that positive affirmation words like *brilliant, outstanding or excellent* affect the recipient. You can quite physically see their body language change for the positive.

To be honest, of all the concepts we introduce in our training programmes, this one consistently gets the most pushback. There are a number of people, it seems, who find the whole idea of positive affirmation a little distasteful. They feel that the words are overdone and the action somewhat disingenuous. I quite understand the concern, but if you're feeling the same way, I will tell you the same thing I tell our trainers to say: don't take my word for it. Don't, for that matter, take my word for anything I say. Try it for yourself and see if you don't notice a profound difference in how people respond to you. If it doesn't work, by all means call me at my office and tell me I'm an idiot. I'm okay with that. But if you actually do try it, I feel pretty safe that you'll end up agreeing with me.

2. 'Absolutely', 'Of course!', 'It would be my pleasure'

The next time someone asks if you can do something, go a step further than just saying 'yes'. These words send the message that, not only will you do it, you're *happy* to do it.

3. 'I want to get this right for you'

If you're asking someone to wait while you look something up

for them, or if you're taking a little more time getting something done than anticipated, this phrase helps turn it into a
positive. It's the difference between: 'Can you give me a minute
while I look this up?' and 'Can you give me a minute while I
look this up? I want to get this right for you.' You'll be amazed
how much more patience people will have with you when they
understand that you're looking after their best interests.

4. Speak in sandwiches

The best way to present negative information or a difference of
opinion is to use good-stuff – bad-stuff – good-stuff language
sandwiches. Say, for example, a co-worker or boss has an opinion that you don't entirely agree with. You could say, 'I don't
entirely agree with that', which is pretty much guaranteed to
make her a little defensive. A better approach would be, 'Susan,
that's a good idea (Good Stuff). If we modified it a little to
address these X issues (Bad Stuff), I think it can really work. I
think you've really almost nailed it (Good Stuff)...' With this
approach, Susan will be less defensive, and more receptive to
your ideas.

5. Words of empathy

I suspect most of us have first-hand experience that life doesn't
always go quite as smoothly as we would like – and that sometimes the twists that life throws at us can be very, very stressful.
When times get tough, our focus naturally turns inward, and
it's not unusual for people during these periods to feel alone
and besieged. It is at moments like these that we appreciate
empathy the most. We don't necessarily want someone to solve
our issues (although that would sometimes be nice), but it's
nice to know that someone grasps the implications of our
situation.

To have empathy with other people doesn't mean you have to fawn over them or gush. You just have to let them know that you understand and care about what they're going through. When it comes to creating connections, there is no stronger message that you can send. One of the most powerful sentences you can have in your communications toolbox, in fact, is: *'From what you've told me, I can understand why you're frustrated'* ('frustrated' can be replaced with 'angry', 'upset', or similar appropriate words). It says to the person that you've taken the time to listen, and that you recognize their emotional state. You're not necessarily agreeing with them, you're just empathizing with them.

26

Networking

If you're always there for other people,
you will never face challenges alone

Here's an all-too-common scenario: Joe gets laid off from his job of 10 years, and now finds himself looking for work. He follows the standard advice from employment gurus, and begins his search by trying to tap into his personal network. The only problem is that, over the past 10 years, Joe has never actually taken the time to build his network. So, the next thing you know, he's sending e-mails and making phone calls to people he's only ever met once or twice in his life, asking them for help. In doing so, he comes across as self-serving and disingenuous. The strategy rarely works.

The importance of keeping a strong, active personal and professional network can't be overstated. Perhaps nothing speaks more directly to the importance of connecting with the people around us than the concept of networking. When you look at high achievers in virtually every industry, you will find that they have all developed a very strong group of people around them. The more jaded among us attribute their successes to 'the old-boy's clubs' and 'politics', but in reality these terms are just cynical, sour-grapes labels to describe the success of people who understand the principles and power of networking.

It is a truism that people prefer to deal with people they like, and want to help people they like. It only makes sense, therefore, that the more people you get to know, the better off you'll be. (Assuming, of course, you're a likeable person.) It's a lot of work to build a strong personal network, but the ultimate payoff is tremendous. The following are the absolute musts of networking. Many we have already discussed elsewhere in this book, but they are part of networking and bear repeating.

1. Connect people

The secret to building a network, as any networking expert will tell you, is to do things for other people, not ask them to do things for you. Here is the simplest and most powerful piece of networking advice you can ever have: be a connector. If you know of a good software developer, and know of somebody who's looking to have software developed, pass the name along. If you know someone who is selling something and someone who is looking to buy, hook them up. It doesn't matter how important you think these people might be to your future – if you genuinely think the match is right, connect them.

Every time you make a connection, you're helping two people at a time, and the message you send is that you're thinking about them, and that they're important to you. Make this a regular practice, and you'll find that when the time comes that you need your network, it will be there for you.

2. Laugh

Be someone people can turn to to cheer them up when things are going sideways. The greatest enemies of misery are hope and laughter. If you can give those things to people, you become a very valuable commodity indeed.

3. Be a source of information

Become an insatiable reader and gatherer of knowledge in your subject area or your industry. Become the 'go-to' person when people have a question.

4. Be involved

Get involved in charities, volunteer organizations and not-for-profit events. Position yourself as someone who is involved and engaged.

5. Remember

Most of us know at least one individual who can seemingly remember every detail about the people they meet. They remember your name, where you were born, the name of your spouse, etc. They stand out in comparison to most of us who often just can't remember one person's name within moments of being introduced. It's a remarkable skill, and a sure-fire way of winning people over in a hurry.

How can you develop this valuable talent? There are a number of memory courses available, and they will tell you that it really boils down to how closely you pay attention in the first place, and how well you organize your thoughts as you store them in your brain. They work, but if you just don't have confidence in your own grey matter, you can instead try a technique that professional salespeople have been using since the beginning of time: cheat sheets.

Good professional salespeople keeps extensive and relevant up-to-date contact information on their customers and potential customers. They record the details of their interactions, including any peripheral information that might be salient. Prior to a subsequent meeting with that customer, they will then take a few moments to review these notes to prepare. This way, when they see their customer, all of the necessary information is on the tip of their tongue.

If you want to establish yourself as someone with a great memory, but aren't convinced your memory is up to it, try keeping notes on your interactions with the people around you. Then the next time you're going to a function, brush up on your information about them and show up prepared. (You don't want to be collecting too much or too personal information on someone, of course. You don't want to come across as some psychotic stalker, or an MI5 or CIA wannabe.)

6. Be a mentor

Most of us know how much of a difference a mentor can make to our success. Mentors are important, because they lend expertise, support and a different perspective to our endeavours. It's important to recognize, however, that being a mentor is just as important as having one.

Be on the lookout. And whenever a mentorship opportunity comes up, seize it. When someone is looking for guidance or input on an area that you're good at, help them out. Not only does your 'student' benefit, but you will find that the process of teaching will also improve your own understanding of things. It's a very rewarding process for everyone.

Just a few notes about mentoring:

a. You don't have to be in a position of power to mentor someone. You just have to be knowledgeable and caring.

b. Don't try to mentor in areas that aren't your strong suit – don't 'wing it'.

c. Never, ever impose your 'mentoring' on others. If someone has asked for your help and expertise, then you're a mentor. If you're volunteering it without being asked, you're just being opinionated, and you're probably not helping.

d. People ask for your help because they trust you. Don't ever betray that trust.

e. Don't ever take the things your student says lightly. If they brought it up, it's important to them.

f. Never forget that it is all about the other person.

Try it! There's something to be said for going to bed at night knowing that you've made a difference in someone else's life. If you do it well, the people you mentor will ultimately be the most valuable people in your network.

7. Be there for the 'little people'

I mentioned earlier the age-old wisdom that says you can gauge someone's character by the way they treat a waiter or waitress in a restaurant. The same philosophy applies equally well when looking at the way we treat others in the workplace –

particularly those internal service providers occasionally referred to with tongue in cheek as the 'little people'.

Many of us will often spend great energies trying to impress or gain positive attention from the more powerful people in an organization. But when the little guy needs help – the part-time employee, the janitor, the clerk, the junior team member – we're suddenly nowhere to be found. The way you treat the people around you, at all levels, really does make a huge statement as to how well you fit into a team. From a networking perspective, you don't ever want to alienate anyone, regardless of who they are. Besides, you never know when you might need one of the 'little guys' in a big way.

Social networking

Undoubtedly the fastest-growing aspect of networking continues to be the tsunami of social media such as Facebook, LinkedIn, Twitter, etc. When this phenomenon first began, there was a strong general opinion that it was just a fad restricted to teenagers, and would never take root in the business world.

Wrong.

Social media has become ingrained in our culture, and is now an absolutely necessary networking tool. It allows you to be completely up to speed in virtually every facet of your business, and the applications of this technology have only just scratched the surface. They are used for job searching, recruitment, background checks, competitive information and just good, old-fashioned meeting new people with similar interests. If you don't have a LinkedIn or Facebook account, open one. Don't worry if you don't know what to do with them right away – you'll learn. Look for opportunities to help other people out. The same with Twitter. Open an account, and find some people who are relevant to your career and follow their tweets. You can learn an awful lot just by keeping your eyes and ears open.

Networking, when done properly, has a remarkable effect. The more you pay attention, and the more you selflessly help the people around you, the more frequently exciting things magically begin to happen for you. It's not really magic, of course, nor is it coincidence. You just have to be consistently aware of your surroundings, think about what you can do for others (instead of what they can do for you), and believe, yet again, that what goes around truly does come around.

Part 5

Dealing with stress and difficult people

People who have the skill to deal with difficult situations are extremely valuable to their organization

I left this section to the end for a reason. You see, if you focus on doing the things we talked about in the first parts of the book, you'll just find that stress points and difficult people become rather few and far between. Although the more cynical among us may take issue with this assertion, the indisputable facts are that:

- friendly people don't get yelled at as often;

- people who work hard don't get as much abuse from bosses;

- people who are always there to help out don't have as many issues with co-workers;

- people who have empathy don't have as many customers from Hell;

- people with a positive attitude don't get as stressed;

- people with great skill and a strong network don't get passed over for promotions;

- people with a plan encounter fewer roadblocks.

It really is that simple. For the most part, the impact that stress and difficult people have on us is largely negated by a winning attitude and positive work practices.

Having said this, however, even in the most positive of workplaces negative things can happen. And your ability to address these positively, proactively and effectively will go a long way to enhancing your job satisfaction and your career path. In the following two chapters, we explore the basics of how to deal with people when difficulties arise, and how to deal with the stresses in today's workplace.

27

Difficult situations and people

No one in the history of humanity has ever calmed down after being told to calm down

When I wrote the *Winning with the... from Hell* book series (*Winning with the Customer from Hell, Winning with the Boss from Hell, Winning with the Employee from Hell and Winning with the Caller from Hell*), I did a tremendous amount of research into the reasons why otherwise good people can sometimes behave so badly. What I discovered was that in almost all cases, there was a common progression of events that went like this:

1. Expectation. The other person has an expectation of you, your team or your department.

2. Issue. Something goes sideways, the person discovers that the expectation is not or will not be met, and raises the issue to you.

3. Response. You respond to what the person says.

4. Conflict. The way in which you respond triggers a negative emotional response from the other person.

5. Confrontation. The person's negative emotional response triggers a negative emotional response back from you.

The first two stages are an inevitability in any environment. Someone expects something that is not delivered and says something about it. These types of event happen every day. It's not until the third stage, however, that the potential for an unpleasant situation really materializes. It is this stage that determines the direction and tone of everything to follow. If your response sends a clear signal that you care about the other person and want to try to make things better, the interaction will most often take a positive path. If your response, either intentionally or inadvertently, sends the message 'sucks to be you', then the battle lines are drawn.

It is this critical point, this nexus, that we really need to focus on. Yes, there are many techniques you can employ once things have really gone awry, but by that time, the toothpaste is already out of the proverbial tube and can't be put back in again. It is far better to keep things from getting to that point, and that's what this chapter is all about. The following are four tremendously effective strategies you can employ to short-circuit issues before they head down the road to confrontation.

First Response

When your customer, co-worker, boss or employee comes to you with an issue, the first words out of your mouth are absolutely critical. You need to convey as quickly as you can that you are genuinely interested in trying to make things right. Here are two sentences that you simply must commit to memory:

1. Let's figure out how to make this work.

2. Let's see what we can do.

Let's take a look at some examples of how people might respond to different issues. The first represents the more common response you might hear. The second uses one of the phrases above:

Boss: (Issue) Fred, I just looked at this project and we are seriously over budget.

Fred: (Wrong response) It couldn't be helped. There were a lot of unexpected expenses...

Fred: (Better response) Wow, it sure is. Let's see what we can do...

Co-worker: (Issue) Susan, there's no way we're going to get this done on time.

Susan: (Wrong response) Well, we better, or the boss will have a fit.

Susan: (Better response) It does look pretty bleak. Well, let's figure out how to make this work.

Customer: (Issue) What do you mean you don't have enough in stock? I need these right now!

Fred: (Wrong response) I'm sorry, sir, but that's all we have.

Fred: (Better response) Let's see what we can do here...

Employee:	(Issue) Boss, it looks like we have a problem...
Susan:	(Wrong response) WHAT??!!
Susan:	(Better response) Well, let's figure out how to make it work.

In each of these scenarios, the 'Better response' strategies communicate the desire to reach a positive solution. It's easy to see how the other person's reaction is far more likely to be positive than when the more common strategies are used. It doesn't matter at this stage whether or not you actually *can* create a positive outcome. What is important is that you've communicated that you genuinely want to try to find one.

These first responses make intuitive sense, and genuinely make a profound difference to the intensity and duration of any conflict that may follow. The biggest obstacle that you will encounter, in fact, is likely to be your own pre-existing bad habits. You see, most of us, when faced with an issue, instinctively take a defensive position. We look for excuses ('Yabut...'); we try to shift blame ('It's not my fault...'); we push back ('You never told me...'); and so on. In order to prevent this from happening, you have to find a way to program the positive first response as the default into your brain. In our offices, we have posters that say 'Yabut *Let's figure out how to make this work*' in front of every desk. It helps remind us always to begin on the right foot.

Confirm, Clarify and Continue

A remarkable proportion of conflict is caused by misunderstandings and misinformation, followed by someone making someone else feel stupid. Take this as an example:

| Joe: | I've taken a look at your computer – it's going to take about a day to fix. |

Sally:	A whole day? No, you can just swap the drive out like you did for Fred's computer.

Joe (Wrong way): This isn't Fred's computer, now, is it?

or

Joe (Wrong way): Actually, no I can't.

or

Joe (Wrong way): That's not going to do it.

Joe's statements, while perhaps true, are almost guaranteed to push one of Sally's cold buttons. They are confrontational, and leave Sally no choice but to either argue the point, or accept that she's stupid. Neither of these is a productive outcome.

The Confirm, Clarify and Continue strategy is an effective way to clear up misconceptions while at the same time minimizing the potentials for conflict. As the name suggests, it has three components.

Confirm

When you look closely, you'll find that most misconceptions are grounded with at least some seed of truth. If you make the effort to look at things from the other person's perspective, you can usually figure out where the misunderstanding occurred. The Confirm part of this strategy is where you acknowledge this, to communicate that you don't believe they are stupid for having thought that way.

Going back to our example, then, it might look like this:

Sally:	A whole day? That's nonsense. You can just swap the drive out like you did for Fred's computer.

Joe: I can understand how it can look that way.
                        On the surface, the issue appears very simi-
                        lar.

Clarify

This is the part where you set the record straight. Try to do it
without using the word 'but.' For example:

Sally: A whole day? That's nonsense. You can just
                        swap the drive out like you did for Fred's
                        computer.

Joe: I can understand how it can look that way.
                        On the surface, the issue appears very simi-
                        lar. In your case, it's actually not the hard
                        drive, it's the motherboard that is causing
                        the problems, and that takes a bit more work
                        to replace properly.

Continue

The Continue part of this technique is the key – and the one
that helps to ensure that the issue quickly becomes a non-issue.
It all has to do with understanding conversation flow and
control.

In normal conversation, we take cues as to when it is our turn
to speak, and leave cues to signal other people it is their turn to
speak. It is these subtle conversation cues that create conversation dynamics. When you are finished speaking you might,
for example, signal people it is their turn with silence, a question, a hand gesture or shift in body posture. The nature of
how you finish tells others how they are to proceed. If you ask
a question, they answer. If they look at you with their head

tilted to one side, they may be looking for your agreement or explanation, etc.

In conflict conversations such as these, we often fall into a pattern of 'making points'. I make my point, then you make your point, then we continue back and forth hoping that one of us will eventually concede. It's a pattern that has to be broken in order to move forward in any conflict.

With this pattern in mind, then, imagine the result if Joe just stopped after he had clarified the issue: '... and that takes a bit more work to replace properly'. Based on the traditional conflict pattern, it's now the other person's turn to speak. What will she talk about? You guessed it – she will return to the issue.

What Joe needs to do is move the conversation beyond the issue, and he can do that by asking a question. See what happens when he actively tries to move the conversation forward:

Joe: I can understand how it can look that way. On the surface, the issue appears very similar. In your case, it's actually not the hard drive, it's the motherboard that is causing the problems, and that takes a bit more work to replace properly. *Is there any critical data you would like me to transfer to another machine so that you can work on it while I'm getting this fixed?*

Joe has now moved the conversation to a decision as to what data Sally might need to work on while the computer is being fixed. The issue and potential conflict as to whether or not the problem is the same as Fred's computer is a distant memory.

Feel, Felt and Found

There are times that you will find yourself in a position of having to defend a policy or protocol that someone else simply doesn't agree with. Take, for example, a co-worker who needs access to a confidential document, but you can't release it until your boss has signed off on it. You might hear: 'This is ridiculous. I've been working here for 10 years. How am I supposed to get my job done when I can't get the things I need?'

This is deer-in-the-headlights time for most people, who will grope for something to say, then end up responding with some variation of 'I'm sorry, but that's our policy.' *Instant* conflict. You might as well have actually said the words, 'sucks to be you'.

The Feel, Felt and Found strategy is a time-honoured method for empathizing and introducing different perspectives with a minimum of conflict. Here's how it might sound as applied to our example:

'I know how you feel. I have to get him to sign off on my stuff too, and I felt exactly the same way when I was in your situation. What I found, though, was that he can often keep a lot of things from going sideways when he's in the loop like this. It's a huge frustration, but it ends up making a lot of sense.'

In this example, you can see how the empathy works in the 'Feel' and 'Felt', and how well it positions the reframing in the 'Found' part. Like the Confirm, Clarify and Continue technique, it won't work all the time, but it works better than any other approach I've heard.

Say No Nicely

Some of the biggest challenges in the work environment are

those times when you have no choice but to say 'no' to some-one's request. Sometimes it's because of a firm and non-negotiable policy that is in place. Sometimes someone is looking for something you just don't have. And, of course, sometimes what he is asking of you is just plain unreasonable. It's tough, because the whole concept of saying no seems counterintuitive to the philosophies we've discussed so far. But the reality is that you simply can't always give everyone what they want. Sometimes you have to stand your ground.

So the question becomes, how do you say no in a way that minimizes the potential for conflict? There's no perfect way, of course. But here's one strategy that works very consistently:

1. **Express regret and empathy.** Say something like, 'I really wish I could', 'I'd like to', 'I can see why this would be important to you', etc.

2. **Explain the reasons why you can't accommodate their request.** (Avoid the words 'policy' and 'process'.)

3. **Look for alternatives.** Say something like 'let's see what we *can* do'. Let them know that you want to try to help.

This simple strategy lets the other person know that, while you might not be able to give them what they want, you're willing to work with them to try to get them what they need. Make sure to ask them a lot of questions so you know the real purpose behind their request. The better you understand where they're coming from, the easier it will be for you to find a workable solution.

'What about win–win solutions?' you may ask. Shouldn't we be looking for those? Fair question. To be honest, I'm not completely sold on the concept of win–win. Oh sure, when it's attainable, it makes all the sense in the world. I'm just not convinced that it's really attainable as often as we'd like. A lot of the time, maybe even most of the time, no matter how hard you try to spin it, someone's going to lose. I think a more effective approach is to replace win–win with fair–fair. In those awkward situations, when people aren't going to be able to walk away with what they wanted, you at least want them to walk away feeling that they were treated fairly.

These four strategies, First Response, Confirm, Clarify and Continue, Feel, Felt and Found and Saying No Nicely are very powerful tools to have in your toolbox. Combine these with all of the positive interaction strategies in the beginning of the book, and there will be very little that comes your way that you can't handle.

Change your priorities

One last thing about dealing with difficult people. Imagine the following scenario: you're in a meeting with 10 people, and one of them decides to argue a point with you. You reaffirm your position, and the person becomes overtly belligerent. His behaviour is confrontational and his position unreasonable. What do you do? Do you become more aggressive and stand up for yourself? Or do you back down to end the confrontation? You want to find a way to get along, but that just doesn't appear to be an option. It's time for a shift in conflict management strategy.

Sometimes, no matter how skilled you are or how hard you try, you can find yourself in a public situation with someone seemingly bent on being miserable. It's at times like these that your focus has to change from 'what can I do to resolve this situation', to 'what can I do to ensure I'm positioned in the best light *to the other people around us*'. In the scenario above, there are nine other people in the room. One of them has made it perfectly clear that you are not going to have a positive relationship. The only 'win' you can hope to achieve is to ensure that the remaining eight people don't think you are as crazy as the other guy.

To do this, you have to do everything in your power to create as great a contrast as you can to the other person. The more unreasonable he gets, the more reasonable you have to appear. The more wildly he makes his points, the more deliberatively you make yours. Your goal is not to 'win' the current interaction, but to win the hearts of everyone else. It's a remarkably effective strategy, and you will be very pleased with how it impacts your image in the workplace.

28

All stressed up and nowhere to go

Don't look for problems. It takes neither courage, nor imagination nor brains to find problems. Problems have a way of finding us

Do you feel as though the overall stress levels in your workplace seem to have escalated over the past 10 years or so? I don't think it's your imagination. Requests for my company's internal customer service and workplace development programmes have tripled in the past three years. Every year, over a million people 'Google' workplace stress-related search terms such as difficult situations, difficult people, bad bosses, mean co-workers, nasty customers, etc. Nope, if you're feeling stress, you're not alone. More and more research is pointing to stress as a growing factor in all of our lives.

One study released in 2007 (*Voices of Canadians: Seeking Work–Life Balance*, by Duxbury, Higgins and Coghill) confirmed that stress at work is negatively impacting us both at work and at home. Similar studies in the UK, United States,

Australia and other countries show that the escalation of stress is a worldwide phenomenon.

In theory, if you are able to adopt the winning attitude, then negative stress shouldn't end up playing a large role in your life. But stress has a funny way of sneaking up on us, and it's good to be prepared when it rears its ugly head. Here are six strategies you can use when you start to feel a little overwhelmed. The first two come from the Duxbury, Higgins and Coghill study.

1. Put things into perspective

Learn to recognize what (if anything) is truly worth losing sleep over. In the overall scheme of things, is this a life-changing event, or just an annoyance? Learn to ignore the annoyances.

2. Focus on what is going well – not what is stressful

At any given moment, something in your life is going right (honest – it is!). Concentrate on the wins in life, not the losses.

3. Identify your cold buttons

If you haven't already, take the time to write down the things that consistently push your buttons. Ask yourself why these things bother you so much. Sometimes just by identifying the source of your emotions you can start to beat them. If you've already done this exercise, dust off your list and re-read it.

4. Focus on the issue

Make an effort to stay focused on solving the situation. Most often, it's the emotions attached to the situation, not the situation itself, that are causing the feelings of stress. Push the emotions to the back of your mind, set a goal, and take action.

5. Create a ranking system

A lot of times we find ourselves getting upset about things that don't really warrant the effort. Ask yourself, on a scale of 1 to 10, 'How critical is this to my life?' Come up with something to use as the benchmark for a '10'. That way you have something concrete to compare it with. If a 10 on your stress-o-meter, for example, is 'death by falling into a giant blender', then the current unemployment situation you may be facing suddenly doesn't seem quite so bad.

6. Create a new morning routine

Chronic workplace stress typically begins at the start of the workday, then escalates as the day progresses. Interrupt the pattern by creating a new morning routine. Go to a different place for your coffee. Do your administrative work before you check your e-mails, etc.

Conclusion

It's too late to wait until tomorrow to decide whether or not you should have been happy yesterday

I have two questions.

It would appear that the number of people actually enjoying themselves at work is continuing to decrease at a steady and alarming rate. Even worse is that many of us can't even imagine having fun at work. Suggest to someone that work should be an enjoyable place, and there's a good chance you'll be met with scornful laughter. 'I don't know what you're smoking', I've heard more than one cynical voice say, 'but I need some of that.'

On one hand, I find this trend most disturbing. Work shouldn't be a penance. On the other, more mercenary hand, I console myself with the knowledge that as long as people insist on making the lives of themselves, their customers and co-workers miserable, I'll never be out of work.

Two good friends of mine recently turned down tremendously prestigious CEO positions with salaries that would make a professional athlete blush. Interestingly, they both had the same explanation: they were enjoying the jobs they had, and the extra money wasn't worth the increase in stress. One mutual acquaintance shook his head in bewilderment, saying, 'Man, these guys just don't get it.' I, however, think they do get it – better than most of us.

There's the age-old question, 'Do you work to live, or live to work?' My first question, however, is, why not live while you're at work? When you do the maths, you'll find that you actually spend more of your life at work than you do anywhere else. If you're not enjoying yourself, then what's the point? There are way too many of us out there that take ourselves way too seriously. Should you take your work seriously? Of course you should. But nowhere is it written that serious work has to be miserable work.

Highly successful people – those with the winning attitude – are able to look at the individual events in their lives from a positive perspective. They can look back at their career paths and see how almost every twist and turn, every challenge they faced, in some way helped them get to where they are. Sometimes an event steered them in a different direction. Sometimes it forced them to see things they hadn't seen before. Sometimes, it was just a very painful part of the learning curve.

My second question, then, is do we really have to look back on something in order to appreciate it? Wouldn't our whole life experience be better if we made the effort to find the positives in things today? Yes, I recognize that it sounds terribly idealistic, but how could it hurt to try?

Success at work, however you choose to define success, is there for the taking. All it takes is a winning attitude and the application of some fundamental principles that are achievable for everyone. Maybe the best part is that we can *all* win at work.

There are no losers in this journey – only those who don't pack their bags and get started.

Bon voyage!

Poetry for the
Newly Single
40 Something

To Mary,
It's lovely to work with you
and I'm always here to help
as you keep going forwards
With love
Maria

Maria Stephenson ✗

Stairwell Books

161 Lowther Street
York, YO31 7LZ

Poetry for the Newly Single 40 Something©2017 Maria Stephenson
and Stairwell Books

ISBN: 978-1-939269-59-1

Second printing

Printed and bound in UK by Russell Press
Layout and cover design: Alan Gillott
Cover photography: Sue Coates

Dedicated to my two sons, who journeyed with me
with thanks to family and friends, always there
and to Michael, for whom I will only ever write happy poems.

Table of Contents

Caterpillar

Time slips by, days much the same
though a hunch that more may exist.
This burdened life is all I know,
feeling vulnerable and at risk. ⁄⁄

Till Death Do Us Part

Come, read the inscription;
here reside my remains,
the shadow of who I was
before breath was pressed from me,

leaving me rigid
through lack of movement,
surrounded by the stench of my fear.
I feel your stare,
at the memory of me
as I gaze into nothingness.

I listen as you go on without me
and beat upon these walls;
thrashing in despair,
wailing into empty air;

no mercy is afforded.
pausing, I hear
another thudded nail,
crushing me deeper
beneath the surface;
then silence.

I reach forth into darkness
to which my eyes
have grown accustomed.

Will I be hauled out in time
or am I here forever?
Constrained within
the coffin
of my marriage. ⁄⁄

Lined Up Empties

Splayed plastic can rings, discarded
like spent knickers beside
a yellow trail from misaiming at
the toilet beside a residual stain
of spewed liquor

mingled with morsels
from your culinary attempts.
Charred pans, congealed remains
burns, butts
and your empties
lined up like ghouls.

Your mind will conceal reminders
of your frayed ranting
prior to passing out where you remain
in a state of collapse,
your worn face stained like decaying teeth,
emitting beer-soaked breath
into your drool-drenched pillow
until you emerge
to relive yesterday today
and again tomorrow. ⁄⁄

Daydreams

are the slices of light that permeate
through the clouds that shadow,
haunt, then devour me.

They are oaths of times that beckon
and strength I will gain
with peace that
will fold its arms around me.

I want to reach up and feel them;
hold them in my hands
so that no one can wrench them away.

They are the colours that bow towards me
then whisk me away for a while,
giving a glimpse of what I'll become,
who I should be.

The figment of my thoughts,
the object of my promises
a blissful place to pause.

I dream today what I'll live tomorrow
once I've found courage to fly from here. //

The Dividing Wall

Crouched, cat-like,
your car on the drive,
my insides contract
as I cross the threshold,
sensing your presence
in every pore
of what should be
a place of calm.

The debris of pizza,
discarded shoes,
a hint of
cigarette smoke.
Looking in the mirror,
I'm shocked at
the creased forehead,
and stone-set mouth.

An overhead creak
causes panic,
a throat clearing
I can't bear
then a rhythmic snore
takes hold,
vibrating through
paper walls.

I scrunch in
my makeshift bed
next to our
dividing wall,

seething. ⁄⁄

Only Because I Love You

Some say I'm a hostile host,
preferring us to be alone.
I don't wish to share you, but
it's only because I love you.

Clothing only of my choosing,
cosmetics not necessary,
you'll look as I allow, but
it's only because I love you.

At home where you belong,
Staying, waiting for me.
Pastimes by my side, but
it's only because I love you.

At times you try to defy,
sculpt a life that's free,
and then I'm forced to rein you in, but
it's only because I love you.

You need to rely upon me,
your compliance makes me strong,
you know I'll never let you go, and
it's only because I love you.

You often spur my temper,
I regret when I lash out,
I truly don't like to hurt you, and
it's only because I love you.

To attempt to escape was a mistake,
you could only be by my side,
I had to silence your cries.

It was only because I loved you. ⁄⁄

Ever Decreasing Circles

From the outside, a cosy glow emits,
a blast of warmth when the door's ajar,
when the night is cold she should be tempted,
yet dark and isolation's on a par.

Her footsteps pound a drum into the stillness,
and company is kept with clouds of breath,
towards her home, she tiptoes ever closer,
yet feels as though she's edging towards death.

Without thought, her journey takes a detour
in an attempt to stall the passage home;
the damp pavement sparkles in the shadows,
and she has never been more alone.

Her mind churns over un-kept promises,
she's made to herself and failed to keep
that one day home would be a haven,
more than just a place to sleep. ⁄⁄

Her Mind Will Set Her Free

Curled amongst splinters and dust,
she carves herself a place;
invisible to all,
her voice only heard within herself.

Needing just pen and page,
the noise and bustle wont thieve her thoughts;
no jostles or shoves
could prevent this outpouring of words.

As she burrows into her space,
she won't feel the bone-seeping cold
or the minutes slipping out of grasp,
for she can be anywhere, away from now and here;
her mind will set her free. ⁄⁄

But Yet I am Married

Awaking in an expanse of bed,
a hangover's widow. Another day
of disguise, presenting a persona,
being both husband and wife;
but yet I am married

to the stench of stale beer and tab ends,
who spends afternoons sleeping it off
whilst I escort our son to the barber, then
shiver at his match,
being both mother and father,
but yet I am married

to a voice on the phone that promises
I'm only having a pint,' with our housekeeping,
then has six. I cook supper and dine alone,
mulling over troubles in solitude,
but yet I am married

to a man who resides on another planet,
retires at 8pm, whilst I pass the evening,
before securing the house,
powering off,
parted from others,

but yet I am married. ⫽

My Scenario

A country stroll along a lonely lane,
a lake at peace invites my tears to fall.
Yesterday, I turned fearful and small
of love past and present, and its pain.

It tugged me down throughout my chest,
despondent I became and without hope,
holding it all inside is how I cope.
It lingered till my thoughts found fitful rest.

I comforted myself with words of strength
and how I will survive what could be hurled.
Around my heart the shame and sadness curl,
and tighten as I'm searching for the end.

I dry my eyes although I still feel weak
and of this torment I shall never speak. ⁄⁄

The Nuclear Family

I pause, pensively on the pavement
to pass the time of day
with dad, who douses the car,
tenderly rinsing it in readiness
for their next excursion.

It points down the drive
of their semi, towards the lilt of
Sunday Love Songs, drifting
through the open door, along with
the aroma of bacon, coffee and
family banter. Daughter saunters out:
'need a hand Dad?' Whilst son helps mum indoors.

I meander by that evening; a mellow light
seeps from within.
Framed images depict unity over the decades,
smiling down on them as they cluster together
as one,

or so they want it to seem. I wait, watching
as the façade fades into oblivion, faces
contorted in fury as the worst is withdrawn
in one another.

He peers at the past, yearning for hindsight;
she prays to the future, seeking reprieve
before succumbing to destruction and despair;

I picture them, staring into darkness,
tormented by uncertainty and
rocked by resentment.
Bubbling undercurrents of hatred,
coveting the lives of those who crave theirs.

How much time can smiles hide the tears,
sleeves mask the bruises
and desperate eyes weep behind darkened glasses?
I shuffle along,
thankful that I live in isolation. ⁄⁄

I Hear You

And clamp my hands on my ears,
scarcely able to bear the drone:
rising and falling, mainly rising,
always right,

no room for manoeuvre,
certainly not dispute
as you recite from
the gospel of you.

An opinion
that's not yours equals
nonsense,
invalidity,
ignorance.

I want to scream loud enough
to drown your righteous tones,
shut up! Be quiet! You're wrong!

Except you're not.
You never are. ⁄⁄

The Path of Least Resistance

Following stones and crevices
that he's driven roughshod through,
appearing gentle and placid
yet riding over opposition;
trampling all in his way,
gaining speed as he nears his goal.
Unstoppable, glib, all-powerful,
infiltrating whenever a weakness is found,
shouting louder to be heard.

I've become wise.
Held, for long enough
in this narcissistic grip. ⟋

Deadwood

Jaded and worn, you're wilting before me,
battling with stresses thrust at you,
you've never been cherished
but left to wane

without space to allow shoots to erupt,
deadened leaves envelope your form
as you droop under their weight
and they huddle in darkness around you,

letting no light in, no woes can escape,
all is held inside; if only the numbed foliage
could be stripped back, snapped off and
discarded, enabling new buds to emerge.

I reach forth to free them, crisp and rigid,
becoming powder in my grip,
at first you seem smaller in stature,
more vulnerable and exposed,

yet granted room to grow,
you can tower and shine,
free to sway in a gifted breeze,
breathe what you need, abandon the rest
until you're as good as new again. //

Closing Doors

Loss needles at me as I say goodbye.
Onto these walls, I painted my dreams.
No amount of pain could the colour hide.

A hopeful promise when I first arrived
will be carried forth by another, so it seems.
Loss stabs at me as I say goodbye.

Warmth and comfort may have been mine,
now blinds cover where the sun should stream.
No amount of pain could the curtains hide.

Closing doors for the final time,
trying not to think what might have been.
Loss slices me as I say goodbye.

I recall the shouting that caused me to cry
I yearned to escape, to be safe and at peace.
No amount of pain could the music hide.

The flowers I planted will wither and die,
rotting into the ground before they've been seen.
No amount of pain could the colour hide.
Loss lays me to rest as I say goodbye. ⁄⁄

Starry Night

Tears freeze her cheeks,
darkness wrestles with light,
searching for quiet stillness
but sunshine gives way to night.

Wishes that might have been granted
are fireballs, falling away,
she's mesmerised by their motion
and whispers to them to stay.

Trying to shape what cannot be formed,
to catch what has already left,
like hope that now lives in the shadows,
escaping on the night's crest.

Acceptance that nights can be this long,
if not fought then sadness can grow,
perhaps be swept towards a new dawn,
it's time to let the dream go. ⁄⁄

The Other Side

In cold darkness, I gaze at this closed door
and ponder what might lie beyond its lure;
I haven't been as near and poised before,

so open to success but yet unsure,
my life spent entwined with this turmoil
where sense competes with freedom's fresh allure.

I'm so depended on, I must recoil
and swap stale air for oxygen around
for no more of my years I want to spoil.

I will be grateful that I walked new ground,
one day beholden to the risk I faced
and for fulfilment and the peace I've found.

So this decision, from my gut I've based
this, the final shut door that will be faced. ⁄⁄

Chrysalis

In limbo, paused between two worlds
in the middle of future and past,
knowing the best could be yet to come
and yearning to arrive there, fast. ⁄⁄

White Horses

As they charge towards us,
I yearn for him to take my hand
in the heat of his.
What if suddenly
we were as engulfed in a wave
as I in my longing?

Sensing his need to leave,
I am hypnotised alone,
though stood at his side,
making shapes in stars
I will never
be able to join up.

I return,
watching sunlight
dance on waves
radiating on my face
as I give thanks
for this warmth found alone
now he's passed
through my life. ⁄⁄

The Wave

It washes without warning,
swift, silent,
breaking then carrying me
within its crescendo.
I gulp, hard,
hoping not to drown,
to be devoured;
I will not die, I choose
to allow it to engulf me
for this moment only.
I will be ready for the next one
and will cope.

The pain reminds me
I am alive, but was the joy
worth being rained down
within its weight,
hammered,
closing my eyes,
blinking away images that
threaten to overwhelm?
Striving to remain upright
for I will feel joy again.

The salt stains my face;
my eyes will sting tonight.
but I will sleep
knowing, I will become stronger
with each wave. ⁄⁄

Memoirs of a Newly Divorced Woman

She fears to return to places
yielding association,
instead attempting to construct
fresh memories,
now alone.

She recalls valid reasons for the union's death
yet is more haunted
as happy times bubble back,
dislodging their long-anchored selves.

Gazing at the clouds,
knowing she has time now
to mould and shape them, and
draw in breaths that are just hers

but still yearns
for the warmth of his hand
and his smile
as it once was.

Tears stab behind her eyes,
she tries to blink them away
with recollections of
fleeting togetherness.

The sun has lowered
on the life they shared
and she can only pray
it now rises on hers. //

Indian Summer

It seemed as though behind me,
the grieving process had begun.
First, shock at your passing,
deliberate, yet unforeseen,
tears swamped my eyes,
never far away.

I could hide in shadows
or gaze at clouds,
trying to escape them
but they always discovered me.
I could barely believe you had gone.

But as dawn and dusk
Continued to spool over one another,
I realised I was still breathing
and slowly my smile came back,
I knew I could go on
without you.

Until unexpectedly and uninvited
as quickly as you had departed,

you returned. ⫽

Your Brown Shoes

I imagine you slipping your feet inside
as I recall the moment we chose them.
Are they now worn and spent
and would you shop alone for a new pair,
looking along rows of those that
all appear the same?
They have small, silly names,
laced with plans of occasions and outings,
parties where they'll dance, or travels
on first-class secluded cabins,
carpeted with softness
to sink within, without me.

Why so nostalgic about shoes?
Comfy, large, lived-in shoes.
Because, beside me they walked,
when we were inseparable,
like a polished, new pair of shoes. ⁄⁄

Filling up the Void

A diary,
overcrowded like her mind,
until it's emptied
into a list of things to do,
which is as fulfilled
as dusty films,
and books,
all in a queue.

Gosh, spare time?
Walk the dog, wash the car,
water flowers.
No one to tell
so she'll tell Facebook,
kill an hour.

Fast food and
meals over soon.
Music in the car
to drown
her empty tune.

A mobile phone,
that's constant
like her thoughts.
Occupied till
tiredness holds
her eyelids taut.

Catching up,
calling on,
as though last in a race,
lest she be still
and aloneness
start to fill that space. ⁄⁄

Around the Calendar

I still walk where we walked,
alone, yet not lonely
as I was when with you.
You can no longer intrude
on my thoughts.

I survived Easter,
the time of new beginnings
when it was our end.

As summer was born,
our marriage had died.

Instead of basking
in glorious days,
I hid in confinement
until nights darkened
becoming longer and colder

until nothing could prevent
festivities occurring around me
and a New Year
only heightened my solitude.

I shrugged St Valentine
as commercial nonsense
welcoming cards with my birthday,
planned with precision
no longer spoiled.

Then to look forwards
with the clock
to the end of our road
and the beginning of mine. //

The Quiet House

I'd never go out if I lived here
but wander from room to room
and run my hand over piano keys
merging my words with their tune.

Soothed by a clock's ticking
watching dust dance in sunshine
whilst sipping fresh coffee with cream;
the taste of this place free from time.

No passing traffic to distract me
or neighbours to chime hello,
silence and birdsong are steadfast
and clarity is all I'd know.

Breathing pure air in the daytime,
staring at stars through the night,
comparing my life back – then, to now
before enabled to reach my full height. ⁄⁄

Finding the Words

'A word,' he implored,
he stood by the door
so I told him the truth,
'when I think of you,
it's now without woe,
I had so far to go
until eventually I knew,
as a boat, I'm alone,
moored up, hard as bone,
gazing out at this view,
with those times, I am through.

You once brought me low,
my tears formed a queue
then a day much overdue.
Freed from shackles of woe.
How can love turn to hate,
to indifference and then go?
How does all become nothing
and the old become new?'

Once held taut by a toxic glue,
free now to pause and decide what is true. //

Our Life Together

was like being bound in a copious cloak,
impenetrable, warm, stifling, safe,
bearing down on my shoulders, slowing me,
bestowed when grateful and naïve.

Adorned with sporadic black sequins
which sparkled when catching the light,
yet only at certain angles
for mostly, they kept out of sight.

Ill-fitting and sallower of face,
lead weights sewn into the hem.
Although I tried to discard this cloak,
it became a two-faced friend.

Without it I was disorientated,
but got up whenever I fell
at first, with exposure, I'd shiver,
now it's worn by someone else. ⚏

30

The Absent Father

A Sunday afternoon in McDonalds,
amidst the odour of cheap oil and cheese slices,
conversation impossible
against the bing-bong
of drive-thru announcements
and sing-song customer service!

Father and son mirror
one another; in similar stance,
opposite sides, chewing in silence.
The same thick-set eyebrows
held in concentration
as they connect with everywhere
but where they are.

This state
repeated table after table.
Fathers and sons
'liking' all statuses
except their own.

Sunday strangers
to return again next week. ⁄⁄

Pub Widow

Day after day, you were drawn towards its doors.
'There's more life in the morgue across the way,' you'd say,
when I wanted to join.
I would ponder the contrast between staring
at a coffin lid or into a drained glass.
As the months ran past, I thought to ask.

'Why do you think? You'd drive a saint to drink!'
And you'd slam out with that.

One night I wandered by,
staring at beckoning windows and warmth
emitting onto the lonely street.
Lilting laughter filtered into the darkness as
I strained to glimpse your face
bathed in pub light
and drunk mirth.

I've still to drink in the morgue,
yet new year took me through the pub's doors.
I was welcomed without you.
Now you're long gone and it's my turn to be invited,
'Can I get you another one?' ⁄⁄

Your Echo

You're in the raindrops
that cool my grief
at losing you;
you're the leaves
I pound underfoot
to escape you;
you're the breeze
coursing through my thoughts,
etched in every pore,
in memories that catch in my throat
before they choke as a sob.

I yearned to find you,
now I'd give my all to forget
your smile, your whisper, your touch.

Wherever I turn, you're there;
you won't leave, except you have;
I didn't want to lose you,
only now, I do. ⁄⁄

A Dawn Embrace

Desolate in darkness, I embark
on my lonely journey
into the unknown

until the quilt of night begins
to lift and wrap itself instead around hills
and my shoulders,

warming me slightly as
chinks of light start to emerge,
casting shards of hope.

Whether to focus on curious shapes in the sky
or striking hues of coral flame,
I cannot decide.

Distracted by fingers of cloud striving to aid
the sun's ascension whilst straining
to preserve its modesty.

Yet it refuses to be concealed
and exerts its influence,
entwining with shadows,
whether they welcome this embrace,
or not. ⁄⁄

When Clouds Burst

I'm sure you've scrambled
a mountain; picked your way up slippery stones,
wrapped against cold, finding foot holes, aware of the threat
of hanging clouds, should they descend further with the command
and the will to throw you off course - to claim you as their own.

Their placements have an air of defiance.
The desperate sun tries to permeate them
but her wintry rays lose hands down.
She can't warm the mountainous shoulders
nor dry the tears that seep into its lap.

The mountain fathoms the content of its own depths
whilst I strain to catch
words whipped away on the wind
that were only ever an echo. ⟋

Yet to Become

what we are destined,
bunched together in darkness,
joining forces in our quest for daylight,

poking heads skyward,
like moles we transcend,
breathing new life
as we emerge

side by side,
triumphant with colour,
casting hope onto all
who notice us,
bringing joy
to those who pause

and affirmation
that winter is now a
distant memory. ⁄⁄

Butterfly

Free to soar above it all,
showing my colours as I stretch my wings,
finally able to take my flight
so happy now, my heart sings.

Questions from a forty-something single male

What size is your home?
Are your tastes expensive?
How well-travelled are you?
Is your bank balance extensive?
Are you clever and kind?
How large are your breasts?
Can I send you a picture
of things other than pecs?
Can you cope alone
or will you be needy?
Do you ooze poise and class?
Can you also act seedy?
Are your kids off your hands?
Won't you be on my case?
Have you got any issues?
Will you give me my space?
What car do you drive?
How big is your ex?
How much do you earn?
Would you like to have sex? //

Her Undoing

Soaking up tears,
un-ordering the wine,
a bag swinging from her arm,
she would never have arrived.

Butterflies calm,
heart-rate slowed,
the black dress on the hanger
and bracelet adorning its box.

No blusher dusted, lipstick unapplied,
no perfume ever sprayed,
lashes uncurled,
hair hanging loose around her shoulders.

Hope not being allowed to shower
as her outfit planned,
that would not be worn,
not this night.

She would un-answer the call,
forget his smile
and never have heard his voice. ⁄⁄

Night Music

Nonchalantly, you glance around,
smoothing dress wrinkles whilst balancing on heels
pressing lipsticked lips and flicking your fringe.

The whirr of conversation passes
through an undercurrent of virility
which lingers as you approach the bar.
Ordering a Pinot Noir,
you dare not meet anyone's eyes
and drum your fingers in time to the jazz
as its notes journey down your spine.

Ignoring the sense of assessing eyes,
you bar-stool-perch and cross your legs
as though waiting to be joined.

'I'll get that,' he responds to your second glass,
his voice as silken as the Pinot.
Without invitation, he pulls himself
onto the stool next to yours.
You notice good shoes and his crisp, white shirt.

A blush creeps up your throat as
he points himself towards you.
As his hand cups yours,
he becomes the tune to your song
and you know you won't be going home alone. ⁄⁄

My Living Bucket List

I have existed four decades, yet not lived,
not plunged through mountains on a zipwire,
still to master a horse and hurtle through dales,
gasp as fireworks cascade, Hogmany style.

Sign my novel in Waterstones,
swim with dolphins as they surge and fall,
a music festival layered in mud,
buy a handbag from a New York store.

View a sunset from under the Eiffel tower,
hold a poem book bearing only my name.
A Mini Cooper in which I can shoehorn my dog,
fall for someone who will return the same.

Walk from home to Windermere,
bask in my garden hot tub, with wine,
a conservatory that I've built myself,
in which to muse, in ten years' time.

Read music and learn an instrument,
view Northern Lights from a steaming lagoon,
be able to speak fluent French,
leap from a plane, in charge of my chute.

Kiss an Irishman in Dublin,
dive with fishes and a supply of air,
go skiing, a cruise and Australia;
for still I've not been anywhere.

I will recollect when I'm fifty,
having ticked all these items away
and draft my next list of dreams to fulfil,
for life is too short not to play. ⁄⁄

Surviving

Once demure,
until her growth obstructed the light.
Three times she's been torn,
root-from-root and displaced.
Waning at first before seeming to fight,
she tilts her face to the sun and says
'watch me.'
As she regains the will to bloom,
she's impervious to the force
of being held back and pruned.
Instead she reaches taller, growing stronger
and more beautiful with each passing year
whilst bees and butterflies clamour
for her intoxicating welcome.
Some are overpowered by her rapid renewal
but she doesn't need to compete
with counterparts.
She can just be herself. ⧸⧸

Leap of Faith

It had to be now.
Assaulted by abrupt air,
I slid
towards the edge.
Trembling,
hardly daring
to look down,
yet not daring
not to.

The view
stole my breath,
filled me with life,
I fell
without decision.
Too frightened
to admire scenery
but afraid
I might miss it.
Fast floating,
with faith
I'd land
softly.

As two years before,
his belongings in bags
he'd bid farewell and I had leapt.
That time, also in freefall,
with eyes closed, yet still landing safely. ⁄⁄

Questions from a Picky Female

If I shivered, would you lend me your coat?
Does your anger stay unspoken?
Would you give me custody of the remote?
For me, would you hold the door open?

Are you in possession of all your own teeth?
And a bit of natural hair?
Are you a pillock – will you make me weep?
Will you start stalking me everywhere?

Will you talk all the time about your ex wife?
Do you bear deep battle scars?
Do you have some drive and have a life?
Are you obsessed with football or cars?

Do you try to keep yourself in shape?
Are you able to rock a sharp suit?
When the shit hits the fan, can you find your own way?
Are you handsome, tidy and cute?

Can you iron and cook for yourself?
If I say no, will you persist?
Why are you even on the shelf?
Do you really even exist? ⁄⁄

Bubbles

Each carrying
its own gentle
light,

bringing a
rainbow as its
journey takes
flight.
A friend or a
message, good
news with a kiss,
An embrace that
lingers, a star
or a wish.

Spinning fast
in the bubble
as the smiles grow.
Life fizzes
with energy.
Hard to imagine
feeling low.

Happiness becomes
relived and replayed,

Life would
be perfect
if only
it stayed.
Bubbles merge
then join
up with some more.

Will this joy
explode as they
pop on the floor? ∥

These lines on my Face

Each line tells a story. Every new crinkle
becomes a wrinkle with life's advancing pace.
Yes, my brow is slightly furrowed,
tired, etched grooves are somewhat burrowed
but I'm proud of each line on my face.

They show the height of my hurdles,
some cleared, others have bruised.
Outlining wisdom gained through pain,
telling my tale over again.
Each line on my face, I choose.

> So you can keep your creams,
> forget fillers that turn faces
> into something from the Adam's family
> and I will keep this sagging smile,
> at least it's genuine
> like the folds around my eyes
> so you can see my happiness
> and who I really am
> whilst learning who you are.

Each line tells a story. The story of me.
Cruel mother, angry husband, how I became free.
Those tears have long since dried,
there's new adventures to be tried
and fresh lines to be made

as each line tells a story,
mine will tell of faraway places,
loving embraces and a well-kissed mouth
and even after it all heads south,
I'll just call them laughter lines. ⁄⁄

The Sand Timer

The constant flow can neither
be slowed or stopped,
rich in past choices,
former tears and loss.
It can't be turned over,
this life which exists:
a knowing that there's
more to living than this.
Sand pooled below me
can never be
lessened or changed.
I look up
and ahead,
wondering
what
might
remain.
Has
more life
trickled through
than is left behind
or perhaps running out
so I have to find
what happens if I just
let go and be, following dreams,
feeling happy and free.
Instead of looking down, feeling
regret and bereft, I am in control
of the sand that is left. ⁂

Why Bother?

They'll all look the same, in three decades.
From the nose and ears, hair will sprout.
'old age is to blame,' each will declare,
'no wonder my hair is thinning out.'

Good living causes a swelling midriff,
moods that put saints to the test,
waistbands no longer all that forgiving,
a hairy back leering from under a vest.

Hidden in the armchair beneath his paper,
budgie smugglers when off for a swim,
choosing Y-Fronts instead of boxers,
spectacles balanced on leathery skin.

When at best, it's checked shirts and chinos
most men arrive here somehow;
when at rest, it's flannelette PJs
yet we care what they look like now? //

Our Death

It was colder than anything could be,
laid out, there, on the slab.
I had pummeled and poked at it
till momentary movement had been observed
but swiftly rigidity was regained
as rigor mortis set in.
How could something that once roared with life
now be so dead?
At first I beat fists of fury upon its chest
but its heart wouldn't beat again.
I offered promises and prayers
as it peeled away the layers
of what we had become.
Blame burdened my being until
it dragged me behind it.
I couldn't help but stare at its corpse,
returning frequently, crying over it,
wondering how others could breathe life into theirs
whilst I had to seal the coffin lid.
Finally, hopeless tears became hopeful smiles
until the day I clicked the mortuary door behind me,
embracing the sunshine.
And I have never looked back. ⁄⁄

To See Again

What suddenly makes her notice

sunlight as it filters through branches,
a lone bird singing at dawn,
hair, breeze-blown and tousled,
expressions of the forlorn.

A rainbow curving through the sky,
the trudge of an elderly man,
glittering eyes of a child,
dewdrops that dazzle on grass.

Smiles on passers-bys' faces,
the conifers' scent after rain,
first shoots poking through undergrowth,
pictures that gathered clouds make.

The heat of another held close
purity of deeply breathed air,
leaves that crinkle underfoot
an animal's beseeching stare.

Able to feel negative and then let it go
to conjure up love and make it be known.

Is it because of a loved one's passing?
A recovery she's been through?
A husband lost forever,
that helped her become new

and see again? ⁄⁄

Winter Sparkle

This year she will resist the melancholy dark
and catch blissful rays as she walks in the park
from sunlight that dances on the water's surface
then chases spider webs frozen into lace
before relaxing onto bejeweled grass,
reflective from puddles like sheens of glass.

The pavement glitters in the morning light;
branches kissed softly by nature's snow white
as beauty is cast from the pure winter skies,
yet nothing can equal the shine in her eyes.
Even at dusk, her life's lit by the moon;
a smile full of stars makes it feel still like noon. ⁄⁄

Soaring

In contrast with mood,
juxtaposed with jubilant ruby,
he may have foreseen this, yet
his efforts failed.

An unsteady hand,
for once without a pen,
turned to a fresh page
and strode towards it,
robes rustling with movement.
'You've earned this.'
Time to soar. ⁄⁄

The Labyrinth

I could never have imagined that
darkness could become any darker.
Even as, enveloped in despair,
standing at crossroads, alone
and unsure of direction,
not realising that sadness could deepen
and I'd have further in to go.

Then the thud of rockbottom
as I turned and began to tunnel out,
now needing my aloneness,
knowing I could find the exit.

You may not believe me now
when I say I'm grateful for our misery
as now able to fly my own path. ⁄⁄

Two Acres of the Moon can be bought for Twenty Pounds

I'd have to know which part was mine;
I've never been in a rocket.
Perhaps if I acquired a slice of the moon,
I'd book a flight to visit.

Float airlessly, feet never touching down,
wondering how long I could stay;
enjoying the fluttering excitement
before returning to where I'm safe.

To earth, to gaze from afar
and be transfixed by the aura
that illuminates the darkness
feeling apart, yet could always be nearer.

And perhaps that little-owned piece
may never enough fulfil;
I'd need the fullest moon to keep
and all the stars as well. ⁄⁄

Other anthologies and collections available from Stairwell Books

The Exhibitionists	Ed. Rose Drew and Alan Gillott
The Green Man Awakes	Ed. Rose Drew
Fosdyke and Me and Other Poems	John Gilham
Gringo on the Chickenbus	Tim Ellis
Running With Butterflies	John Walford
Late Flowering	Michael Hildred
Pressed by Unseen Feet	Ed. Rose Drew and Alan Gillott
York in Poetry Artwork and Photographs	Ed. John Coopey and Sally Guthrie
Taking the Long Way Home	Steve Nash
Skydive	Andrew Brown
Still Life With Wine and Cheese	Ed. Rose Drew and Alan Gillott
Somewhere Else	Don Walls
Sometimes I Fly	Tim Goldthorpe
49	Paul Lingaard
Homeless	Ed. Ross Raisin
The Ordinariness of Parrots	Amina Alyal
New Crops from Old Fields	Ed. Oz Hardwick
Throwing Mother in the Skip	William Thirsk-Gaskill
The Problem With Beauty	Tanya Nightingale
Learning to Breathe	John Gilham
Unsettled Accounts	Tony Lucas
Lodestone	Hannah Stone
A Multitude of Things	David Clegg
The Beggars of York	Don Walls
Rhinoceros	Daniel Richardson
More Exhibitionism	Ed. Glen Taylor
Heading for the Hills	Gillian Byrom-Smith
Nothing Is Meant to be Broken	Mark Connors
Northern Lights	Harry Gallagher
Gooseberries	Val Horner

For further information please contact rose@stairwellbooks.com

www.stairwellbooks.co.uk
@stairwellbooks